1010 354 orts 97

GARLAND STUDIES ON

# THE ELDERLY IN AMERICA

*edited by*
**STUART BRUCHEY**
UNIVERSITY OF MAINE

A GARLAND SERIES

# ELDERS' VIEWS ON THE RIGHT TO DIE

## FACILITATING DECISIONS ABOUT LIFE-SUSTAINING TREATMENT

CAROL ANN BAER, R.N., PH.D.

GARLAND PUBLISHING, INC.
NEW YORK & LONDON / 1997

**Library of Congress Cataloging-in-Publication Data**

Baer, Carol Ann, 1946–
    Elders' views on the right to die : facilitating decisions about
life-sustaining treatment / Carol Ann Baer.
        p.    cm. — (Garland studies on the elderly in America)
    Includes bibliographical references and index.
    ISBN 0-8153-2675-0 (alk. paper)
    1. Right to die—United States—Public opinion. 2. Aged—
United States—Attitudes. I. Title. II. Series.
R726.B22 1997
174'.24—dc21
                                                            97-487

Printed on acid-free, 250-year-life paper
Manufactured in the United States of America

# Contents

# Tables and Figures

## Tables

## Tables Located in the Appendices

## Figures

# Preface

The growth of medical science in the last twenty years has promoted the use of "life saving" technologies. The elderly comprise over 30 percent of patients receiving dialysis, nutritional support, and mechanical ventilation, and 55 percent of those receiving cardiopulmonary resuscitation (Office of Technology Assessment, 1987). As a result of the increasing availability of life saving technologies to these older patients, clinical and ethical issues have emerged regarding the quality of life, the meaning of postponing death, and the right to choose or refuse such care. Although the benefits and burdens of treatment are viewed differently by individuals, there are no comprehensive measures for health care providers to assess these differences.

The purpose of this study was to describe elderly individuals' current preferences regarding invasive, life-sustaining treatments and to identify their relationship to health, hope and select demographic variables. The convenience sample consisted of 328 adults 62 years of age and older, living in private residences and able to comprehend English.

The design for the study was descriptive and correlational. The investigation was considered correlational since it sought to examine the relationship between hope and/or health status dimensions and life-sustaining technology preferences of elders. A new instrument, the Life-Sustaining Technologies Scale, was developed by the investigator to identify preferences regarding four invasive, mechanical life-sustaining technologies in relation to various functional capabilities. Health dimensions were identified using the Short-Form General Health Survey (Stewart, Hayes & Ware, 1988), a 20 item, multiple choice self-evaluation describing general function and well being. Hope was measured using the Miller Hope Scale (Miller, 1986), a 40 item, six point Likert scale. Data was analyzed through descriptive and parametric comparative statistical procedures. Findings identified preferences of a select group of elders regarding life-sustaining interventions. Generally, elders were more apt to agree to treatment if physically and mentally capable prior to the medical event. Cardiopulmonary Resuscitation was the most commonly agreed to treatment. Health care proxies were designated by 42% of the population to represent their wishes should they suddenly become unable to make decisions regarding their care. There was no direct correlation between hope or health dimensions and life-sustaining preferences.

# Elders' Views on the Right to Die

# Chapter I

# Introduction

## Introduction

The growth of medical science has promoted advancement of many new technologies to promote health and prolong life. Today many individuals are receiving sophisticated technological interventions never before available within the health care environment. These "life saving" resources have become a central component of the treatment protocol in many health care crises. The use of these dramatic interventions often occurs without prior discussion with patients and families. While the development of life-sustaining technologies has saved the lives of many, some survivors and families are raising issues regarding the quality of life and the meaning of postponing death. Related questions of prohibitive health costs, access to care and the right of individuals to choose specific treatments are also being addressed.

Personal health care expenditures for Americans over 65 were projected at $120 billion annually (Pifer & Bronte, 1986). Nearly half of these expenditures were incurred during the last year of life. It was anticipated by the Office of Technology Assessment that the number and variety of new technologies to sustain life will continue to grow in direct proportion to the cost of such technology (Office of Technology Assessment [OTA], 1987). Additionally, costs associated with the initial life-sustaining intervention may be dwarfed by the ongoing expenses associated with survival of patients whose health care needs remain great despite or because of the intervention. For example, it was estimated that the number of elders in persistent vegetative states in the United States was 10,000 (MacKay, 1988) with individual costs as high as $200,000 annually for specialized care.

Although today's technologies are capable of supporting or replacing the function of a vital organ, it is never certain that such treatment will save or restore the life of a particular patient, or if it does, for how long. The quality of life that is sustained may be even harder to predict or evaluate in the context of the patient's unique experience. There is, as a result, uncertainty about how and with whom discussions related to life-sustaining technologies should take place (Emanuel & Stoeckle, 1991). Consumer participation in care is now being defined, however, (Brody, Lerman, Smith & Caputo, 1989; Ende & Kasis, 1989; Moinpour & Teigl, 1989) and the need to solicit and incorporate patients' choices is being recognized (Brody et al. 1989).

**Background**

Self-determination, the patient's right to privacy and the patient's right to refuse unwanted medical treatment are empowering principles supporting legal statutes in this country. There is tremendous uncertainty and anxiety among health providers in determining their legal obligations and permissible range of action and response to these principles. These fears may, in part, be due to varying court decisions on similar cases in different states. It may also be related to the fact that it is difficult for providers to keep pace with the implications of case law for individual treatment decisions as well as the ethical issues related to technological progress.

The patients' right of self-determination was first clearly applied to medical decision-making in a 1914 opinion by Justice Cardozo, in the New York case *Schloendorff v. New York Hospital,* when he ruled that adults of "sound mind" had the right to determine what should be done with their bodies (OTA, 1987). Since the Cardozo ruling personal choice has been recognized as a basic concept underlying a patient's right to be informed about, and to consent to or refuse proposed medical treatments. In addition, the constitutional right of privacy has recently been used by the United States Supreme Court to protect individuals' personal choices regarding medical interventions.

These rights of privacy and self-determination mean little, however, if health care providers do not disclose information necessary for patients to exercise their rights. The reasonable patient or professional practice standard directly supports disclosure by stating that physicians must disclose the diagnosis, prognosis, proposed treatment, alternate treatments, the risks and benefits of all options, and the consequences of no interventions (OTA, 1987). Even the existence of this standard contributes little to consent practices, when health professionals are not committed to the active participation of patients (Beauchamp, 1989). The President's Commission for the Study of Ethical Problems in Medicine and Biomedical and Behavioral Research notes:

> Information is sometimes provided to patients and patients sometime make decisions. But when this happens, and it does not very frequently, the explanation for it most likely does not lie in law, but in medical custom. And we are convinced that this medical custom is deeply ingrained and to date has not experienced much change under the influence of law (1982, Vol. 3, p.320).

The principle of respect for autonomy also identifies the obligation of professionals to disclose information, ensure understanding and foster voluntary decision making. To respect an autonomous agent is to recognize that person's capacities and perspective, including his or her right to hold views, to make choices, and to take actions based on personal values and beliefs (Beauchamp, 1989). Despite the emphasis on patients' rights, a Congressional Advisory Committee noted that the doctors neither routinely acknowledge the patient's right to autonomy nor integrate the patient into the clinical decision making process (1987). Decision making by doctors for patients remains the basis for hospital care (President's Commission for the Study of Ethical Problems in Medicine and Biomedical and Behavioral Research, 1982).

As a result, little is known about patients' assessment of the choices and subsequent actions relative to personal values and life plans. As long as health professionals do not understand " . . . what patients really want for themselves and learn to translate this into clinical acts, autonomy will remain an empty concept" (Hastings Center, 1987, p.10). Exploring patients' views is difficult when these views involve life and death decisions and potential values conflict. Degner notes that prolonging life is particularly worrisome to older individuals. The common statement, "I don't fear death; I fear dying," reveals this anxiety (1988).

Combined with the fact that the elderly are most likely to receive life-sustaining treatments, but least likely to have their treatment preferences honored (OTA, 1987), these fears warrant attention. The ability to keep patients alive beyond what was once considered the point of death is also a progressive drain on available human and material resources. It often results, for example, in costly chronic care facilities designed exclusively for patients who are permanently dependent on life-sustaining equipment (Pifer, 1986; U.S. Department of Health and Human Services, 1989).

Tension in the health care system regarding the use of life-sustaining technologies and the potential implications of dependency, represent the ultimate challenge for the practice of human caring. The challenge also provides the opportunity for nursing to actualize the moral ideal of preservation of human dignity. Historically, the nursing profession has emphasized respect for individuals and the importance of patient participation in decision making (President's Commission for the Study of Ethical Problems in Medicine and Biomedical and Behavioral Research, 1982). Nursing's support of patient autonomy and freedom of choice are evident in several conceptual models (Patterson & Zderad, 1988; Murphy, 1983; Parse, 1987; Watson, 1985). These models discuss human interaction and dialogue as essential to understanding the meaning of each individual's unique way of experiencing the world.

Although an individual patient's experience, personal beliefs, and self-assessment of what is best in terms of his or her own values and life plans are recognized as important factors, they are not systematically identified. Patients' decisions which do not coincide with the 'best' medical decisions may be seen as "irrational" by physicians and, therefore, ignored (President's Commission for the Study of Ethical Problems in Medicine and Biomedical and Behavioral Research, 1982). Despite nurses' philosophical commitment to support patients' decisions, they are often hesitant to intervene when the views of doctor and patient differ, reducing advocacy, to "a myth rather than reality" (Bulechek & McCloskey, 1985, p. 344).

There is, however, growing evidence of an alternate view of caring (Cady, 1991; Watson, 1985) that places the physical body and medical technology in the context of the individual patient's beliefs and values. This "transcendent" view of caring may be seen as the antidote for the limited technological view of recent times and creates a new ontology of mind–body–spirit, emphasizing the relevance of the phenomena of choosing and hope.

Implicit in the investigator's approach to identify elders' views of life-sustaining technologies is the nursing profession's responsibility to examine psychosocial and ethical parameters within the culture which may influence current views. Recent developments of patients willfully refusing or withdrawing life-sustaining treatments, raise questions regarding the individual's level of hope and his or her right to make "life or death" decisions. Due to the variation and meaning among life-sustaining treatment choices, their relationships to personal and social characteristics need to be identified (President's Commission for the Study of Ethical Problems in Medicine and Biomedical and Behavioral Research, 1982). Ware notes that the time has come to develop systematic methods for assessing health from the patient's point of view (in press).

Fundamental questions are being raised regarding health status and quality of life for individuals. How "generic" are generic health measures: Can the same measures be used among elderly and non-elderly populations? One of the 1990's most important research agendas is mastering models in which health status refers to health related quality of life (Patrick & Elinson, 1984). There is increasing emphasis on developing instruments that monitor differences in individuals' total functional ability and emotional well-being across similar diagnostic/disease groups (Ware, in press). However, no one has looked at antecedent factors such as hope, perceived health and demographics which may play a part in individuals' treatment choices.

Therefore, the goal of this research will be to focus on identifying individuals' preferences in the context of their hope attitudes and health status. Research in this new and relatively unknown area will demonstrate the integration between the nursing profession's philosophical values and scholarly scientific work by extending its boundaries of knowledge while developing its ethical foundation (Jameton & Fowler, 1989). It will also demonstrate the role of nursing in empowering clients to articulate their preferences regarding life-sustaining technologies (ANA, 1988).

## Statement of the Problem

This study has been designed to investigate patients' views on life-sustaining treatment and to assess their value preferences. The purpose of this research is to examine elders' views regarding life-sustaining technologies. The study includes a descriptive analysis of treatment preferences in elders and their relationships to hope, health status and demographic variables.

## Specific Research Questions

Within the context of this study, the following research questions will be answered:

1. What are the hope scores of participants?

2. What is the health status of participants?
3. What are the preferences of participants regarding life-sustaining technologies?
4. Is there a relationship between select demographic variables and stated preferences regarding life-sustaining technologies?
5. Is there a relationship between hope and stated preferences regarding life-sustaining technologies?
6. Is there a relationship between health status dimensions and stated preferences regarding life-sustaining technologies?

## Operational Definition of Variables

The following operational definitions clarify the key conceptual terms and variables in this study:

*Life-Sustaining Technology Treatments:* Life-Sustaining Technology Treatments are mechanical devices or procedures that can keep individuals alive who would otherwise die within a foreseeable but usually uncertain time period. They are identified in the Life-Sustaining Technologies Scale (LSTS) as Cardiopulmonary Resuscitation (CPR), Respirator (breathing machine), Renal Dialysis (kidney machine), and Gastrointestinal Feeding (stomach tube).

*Functional Capability:* Functional capability is the individual's perception of physical, mental, and financial requirements necessary to maintain an adequate quality of life. Functional capability is depicted in five subscales of the LSTS: *Physically and Mentally Capable*; *Physically Incapable* of managing activities of daily living though *Mentally Capable; Mentally Incapable* of managing activities of daily living though *Physically Capable*; *Financially Incapable* of withstanding the cost of care; and, a limited life expectancy due to *Advanced Age.*

*LSTS Score:* The LSTS Total Score is an interval level variable derived from 20 items, each with a six point Likert scale. Responses range from "Very Strongly Disagree" to "Very Strongly Agree" and reflect participants' preferences regarding life-sustaining treatment and functional capability. The LSTS Total Score ranges from 20 to 120.

*Hope Score:* The Miller Hope Scale (MHS) Total Score is an interval level variable derived from the 40 items with a six point Likert scale. Responses range from "Very Strongly Disagree" to "Very Strongly Agree." The score range is 40 to 240, with high scores indicating high hope. Because of wording, 12 of the items are reverse scored to determine the MHS Total Score.

*General Health Status:* General function and well-being is identified through a short-form General Health Status Survey (SF-20) which consists of summated rating scales (Stewart, Hays & Ware, 1988). The 20 items represent the following six health concepts or subscales. *Physical Functioning* is assessed by limitations in a variety of physical activities due to health problems. *Role and Social Functioning* are defined by limitations due to health problems. *Mental Health* is assessed in terms of psychological distress and well-being. The measure of *Health Perception* identifies patients' own ratings of their current general health. *Pain* is included to capture differences in physical discomfort (Stewart, Hays & Ware, 1988).

## Variables and Their Levels of Measurement

There are eight major variables identified in this study. The variables and their levels of measurement include:

*Life Sustaining Technologies Scale Total Score:* An interval level variable derived from a six point Likert scale for a LSTS Total Score. There are also nine subscale scores.

*Miller Hope Total Score:* An interval level variable derived from a six point Likert scale. There are also three subscale scores.

*SF-20 Subscale Scores:* Interval level variables derived from three to six point Likert scales for six subscales defining general health. Subscales were scored by summing the item responses, after recoding some items so that a high score indicated better health. The single-item measures were scored so that high scores indicated better social functioning and less pain.

*Age:* Ordinal level variable derived from three age ranges. Category I or "young elders" was comprised of people 62–69 years of age. Category II or "middle elders" was comprised of people 70–81 years of age.

Category III or "older elders" was comprised of individuals over 82–98 years of age.

*Gender:* A nominal level variable.

*Religion:* A nominal level variable.

*Marital Status:* An nominal level variable.

*Educational level:* An ordinal level variable.


## Limitations of the Study

Three limitations were identified in this research:

1. This study is a cross-sectional design involving the collection of data at one point in time. Results of the study do not apply to trends or changes that may occur over time in peoples' lives.

2. This study identifies participants' treatment preferences through anticipated rather than actual situations.

3. The Life-Sustaining Technologies Scale is a new instrument which has not been previously tested on a large population.

# Chapter II

# Review of the Literature

## Introduction

The purpose of this discussion is to focus on literature related to treatment preferences, hope and life-sustaining technologies. The chapter is divided into four sections. In the first section "choices" in health care from the perspectives of medicine, law, and nursing are discussed. The second section is focused on life-sustaining treatments for the elderly and their relationship to health and hope. The development of procedures to insure patients' medical treatment preferences is reviewed in the third section. In the fourth section, factors influencing preferences are described.

## Health Care Choices

### Medical Perspective

Much of the medical literature on choice has focused on: the physician identifying the options and consequences of treatment; evaluating the diagnostic evidence; weighing the benefits against the harms and costs; factoring in economic, legal and personal considerations; and choosing the option that is "best" (Eddy, 1990). The physician's goal has been to replace the patient's subjective language and expressions of discomfort into the universal categories of biomedicine (King, 1988). This approach often overlooks the impact of illness and treatment on the patient's daily life, psychological state or personal values. Patients' personal preferences and values are "largely absent from clinical practice" (OTA, 1987, p.96). The patient is simply informed about the treatment and acceptance is encouraged. Treatment is

*11*

prescribed and enacted unless there is an objection posed (The Presidents Commission, 1982).

Despite this traditional medical view of physicians making decisions for the patient there is increasing pressure to attend to patients' viewpoints. When decisions involve "the risk of death and the impairment of various capacities, the doctor must see himself as the servant, not of life in the abstract, but of the life plan of his patients" (President's Commission, 1982, Vol. 3, p.75). The impact of illness on physical, mental and psychological functioning is now being recognized as an integral part of health status (Eddy, 1990; Nelson, Hays, Arnold, Kwoh & Sherbourne, 1989).

*Legal Perspective*

There are legal standards governing the disclosure and explanation of medical information to patients. The "professional practice standard" holds that adequate disclosure is determined by professional practice which defines information given to patients according to the medical community's values and goals (Beauchamp, 1989). Disclosure according to the "reasonable person standard", however, shifts the determination of informational needs from the physician to the patient. Adequate disclosure is determined by the significance *any* reasonable person would attach to the information in order to make a meaningful decision regarding the proposed therapy (Beauchamp, 1989). A physician who discloses sufficient information to meet the requirements of professional practice may fail to meet the requirements of the reasonable person standard.

Another standard, known as the "subjective standard", refers to the adequacy of information and is judged in context of the specific informational needs of the individual patient. It encourages professionals to facilitate decision making based on substantial understanding of patients' goals, values, and informational needs (Beauchamp, 1989).

*Nursing Perspective*

Historically, nursing has supported patients' involvement in decision making. There has been great emphasis on respect for individuals' values, the therapeutic importance of participation in health care, and the teaching of good communication skills (President's Commission, 1982). The Code for Nurses reflects the profession's increasing attention to an advocacy role. Conceptual Practice Models have emerged (Patterson, 1976; Murphy, 1983; Parse, 1987) emphasizing the need for human interaction and dialogue in order to understand an individuals' unique ways of experiencing the world. Nurses have a high regard for autonomy and freedom of choice in these "caring" relationships with individuals (Cady, 1991; Watson, 1985). Philosophically, nursing is committed to having health professionals assist individuals in determining the personal value and meaning of illness or disability. This philosophical commitment has not been defined, however, in terms of nursing interventions. "Mere acceptance of views is rudimentary to the complexities embedded in participating with the patient in determining the personal meaning which the experience is to have" (Gadow 1983, p.55).

Ketefian (1989) in reviewing the nursing literature noted the paucity of nursing studies dealing with moral reasoning and ethical practice and concluded that empirical investigations of research questions emanating from value judgments and ethical issues would be of great benefit. Gortner's (1988) Values in the Choice of Treatment Inventory is one attempt to identify the relevance of moral principles to treatment choices with cardiac patients. The inventory is confined, however, to moral principles and description of patient values in the context of family values. Ende and Kasis's (1989) work identified that relationships exist between decision making preferences, health status and patient satisfaction. Benefits associated with increasing patients' participation in care have also been identified: improved disease control; a better quality of life; and, a more satisfactory relationship with the physician (Brody et al., 1989). A screening instrument developed by Degner (1988) demonstrated varying preferences for control in newly diagnosed cancer patients.

The limited research regarding patient preferences is a result of varying definitions, inadequate and multiple instruments, and simplistic methods of data analysis (Emanuel, Batty & Stoeckle, 1991). There is a need to investigate systematically patient perceptions and their relationship to health outcomes.

## Life Sustaining Treatments in the Elderly

*The Elderly*

The elderly population of the United States is growing much more rapidly than the population as a whole. People 65 years of age and over comprised 11% of the United States' population in 1980. It is estimated that the number will grow to 13% or 35 million people, by the year 2000 and 67 million by the year 2050 (OTA, 1987). While longevity has increased, so have the number of years a person lives after onset of chronic disease and disability (Pifer, 1986). Following are some facts (OTA, 1987) which clearly distinguish elders' concerns related to health care treatments:

1. Elderly people are at greater risk of life-threatening illness.
2. Elderly persons who experience a life-threatening illness are more likely to be in a state of compromised health and reduced function that negatively affects their quality of life.
3. Elderly people are more likely to have their ability to make health care decisions temporarily or permanently impaired.
4. Comorbidity and age-associated loss of function more frequently complicate the treatment of life-threatening conditions in the elderly.
5. As a group, elderly people consume the largest share of public health dollars.
6. Elderly persons are more likely than younger adults to have contemplated the meaning and value of their life.

These assumptions support the need to investigate relationships between health perception, preferences regarding life-sustaining technology and the meaning and hope elders ascribe to their lives.

*Life-Sustaining Technologies*

Personal health care expenditures for Americans over 65 were projected at $120 billion annually (Pifer, 1986) demonstrating the "high cost of dying." The costs associated with the initial life-sustaining intervention may be exceeded by the ongoing costs associated with the care of patients who survive. MacKay (1988) estimated there were 10,000 elders in persistent vegetative states in the United States with individual costs for specialized care as high as $200,000 annually.

Technological interventions have changed the very definition of death. Fundamental disagreements are frequently expressed in terms of interventions that "prolong life" versus interventions that "prolong dying." The majority of deaths used to occur at home; by 1984, 61% of all deaths in this country occurred in hospitals. This shift, largely related to available technologies, has created a widespread fear among the elderly not about death but about dying in hospitals (Henderson, 1990).

Cardiopulmonary Resuscitation (CPR) was developed 25 years ago and is a widely used means of restoring and maintaining blood circulation and breathing in a person who experiences cardiac arrest.

Data compiled for the OTA indicate that approximately 61% of hospitalized patients who receive CPR are elderly. Studies in some hospitals reflect higher ages. For example, of 294 patients who received CPR in a Boston hospital from 1981 to 1982, 80% were over 60 years of age (OTA, 1987). Rough estimates indicate that 204,000 to 413,000 elderly persons receive CPR in hospitals annually, and an additional but unknown number receive CPR in the community. Death occurs in 75% to 90% of hospital CPR attempts. Although age alone is not a good predictor of the outcome of resuscitation, the higher prevalence of multiple diseases and decreased level of functioning in the aging markedly and negatively affect outcomes. The use of additional life-sustaining technology to treat complications and injuries are much more common in elderly survivors (OTA, 1987).

Although CPR is often the first thing discussed with families, elderly patients are usually not directly consulted. The reluctance to discuss treatment options may be related to assumptions such as: older patients prefer to have treatment decisions made for them; they are less likely to understand the discussion; and, they are more likely to have hearing and speech impediments that interfere with communication (OTA, 1987). In addition to these often erroneous assumptions, the bias toward resuscitation has been strongly advocated by the medical profession. Due to the medical bias and frequency of CPR, various guidelines, policies and legislation exist to clarify and support decisions regarding the life-sustaining treatment.

The respirator is another major life support system which provides mechanical ventilation to replace normal spontaneous breathing. The lack of sufficient prognostic measures for patients with respiratory failure is apparent (OTA, 1987). Survival, functional capacity, and ventilator dependency are difficult to predict. As a result, the respirator is widely used. Health professionals, however, have identified several examples of inappropriate use of the respirator: patients in their nineties with multiple life-threatening conditions; patients for whom it is known in advance that spontaneous breathing will never be restored and patients who are demented, unconscious or even brain dead. Mortality among hospital patients receiving mechanical ventilation is over 45% and even higher for elderly patients (OTA, 1987).

Dialysis, another available life-sustaining treatment, offers an effective artificial substitute for kidney function. Nearly 91,000 Americans receive some form of dialysis. Almost half the new patients starting treatment in the U.S. are over 55 years of age. Reasonable estimates of the average annual costs of treatment of a patient on chronic dialysis range from $20,000 to $30,000 (OTA, 1987). Survival rates among chronic dialysis patients appears to be related to a number of factors, including age at the time of starting treatment. A national survey found that elderly patients on dialysis assessed their health as poorer than others their age and withdrew from treatment at higher rates. Dialysis was discontinued in one of every six dialysis patients over age 60 versus in one of every 11 of all ages (OTA, 1987).

The high costs and ethical dilemmas related to starting and stopping life-sustaining treatments are major concerns which must be approached individually as demonstrated in the case of an elderly, competent gentleman with progressive kidney disease who experienced early symptoms of kidney failure:

> He and his wife considered a trial of dialysis therapy which could prolong his life, but he decided to accept the natural course of his affliction and stated he did not want this type of treatment. Having exercised his freedom of choice, the man seemed content (OTA, 1987, p. 264).

The use of artificial feeding provides nutritional support via a tube into the digestive tract for people who are unable to swallow, digest or absorb adequate amounts of food and fluids. Though artificial feeding meets a basic human need, it often creates ethical dilemmas when used as a life-sustaining treatment. Accurate information about the frequency of this procedure is difficult to obtain but industry data indicate that elderly patients represented 40% to 65% of the 1.4 million people receiving nutritional support in hospitals and nursing home settings (OTA, 1987).

In summary, there is a wide variety of life-sustaining technologies. Their availability can create conflicts between providers and consumers of health care. "A patient preference that runs counter to the advice of health professionals is often interpreted as 'irrational', and efforts will be made to change the patient's mind or to circumvent the patient's request" (MacKay, 1988, p.139). There is a lack of research that reflects patients' choices.

*Hope*

Hope is described as fundamental to human life—a mental attitude toward the future which recognizes uncertainty but envisages possibility (Miller, 1986). Bloch describes man as a hoping animal manifesting desire for a home which is "not yet" (1970). Hope is a person's most valued, private, and powerful resource which gives meaning to one's world (Miller, 1986). It is an intrinsic component of life which provides dynamism for the spirit (Adams & Proulx, 1975), saving individuals from the consequences of apathetic inaction. Greene, O'Mahoney and Rungasamy describe maintaining hope as a coping task of the chronically ill (1982) where patients perceived themselves in a "winning position" over their illness (Forsyth, Delaney, & Gresham, 1984). Studies of hemodialysis and emergency room patients identified that they frequently coped by "hoping that things will get better" (Jalowiec and Powers, 1981).

Dufault and Martocchio (1985) identified threats to hope in persons with cancer: evidence of deteriorating health; behavior of the family, nurses and physicians; lack of information or ambiguity; a sense of being a burden; spiritual distress; and past negative life experiences. Judith Miller's definition of hope is used in this study:

A state of being characterized by an anticipation for a continued good state, an improved state or a release from a perceived entrapment. The anticipation may or may not be founded on concrete, real world evidence. Hope is an anticipation of a future which is good and is based upon: Mutuality (relationships with others), a sense of personal competence, coping ability, psychological well being, purpose and meaning in life, as well as a sense of 'the possible' (Miller, 1986).

There are disparities in the literature regarding hope's relationship to illness which were attributed to lack of valid and reliable measures (Miller, 1986). The Miller Hope Scale (MHS) was developed to test and systematically measure this concept of hope in individuals. Consequential to the development of the instrument, Miller described three levels of hope (1992). The first and most elementary form of hope is wishing. The second level includes hoping for relationships, self-improvement, and self accomplishments. The third level, hoping for relief from suffering personal trial or entrapment, is hope at its greatest intensity and power. It is used to influence outcomes or create a positive attitude (1992).

Farran explored the dimensions of hope in relation to known variables such as stressful life events, social support and health with 126 community-based, healthy older adults (1990). These findings confirmed that as physical health and mobility decline, older people had more difficulty contributing to society and recognized that many issues of life and death must be faced alone. As a result of this investigation, hope-promoting strategies were developed to enable elders to take ultimate responsibility for their lives. Expression of negative as well as positive feelings was encouraged; authoritative coercion was discouraged; and the meaning each individual attaches to a particular event was identified (Farran, 1990). Despite recent investigations regarding hope, there are no published studies identifying elders' hope levels, and their relationship to health or preferences regarding life-sustaining technologies. Although the elderly have been identified as at risk for loss of hope (Miller, 1992), the extent of these losses has not been assessed.

*Multi-Dimensional Health*

Conventional wisdom says that physical, mental and role performance activities decrease as people get older. Many studies focus on the relationship between functioning and disease (e.g., Meltzner, Carman & House, 1983, Rice & Cugliani, 1980). Although there is recognition of variation in functional ability in individuals of advanced age (Ware, in press), only a few studies have measured limitations in activities of daily living with aging (Nelson, 1989; Parkerson, Gelbach, Wagner, Janes and Clapp, 1981). Cassileth (1984) and Feinson (1985) evaluated the relationship between emotional functioning and age and disproved the perception of deterioration in physical function with age. Koenig concluded that "there is greater support for a decrease in frequency of mental disorders among older persons and an increased ability to cope with major life changes when compared with younger age groups" (1986, p. 384).

## Procedures to Insure Patient Preferences

Courts have recognized the uniform applicability of the fundamental rights of patients in medical decision making. The challenge has been to develop procedures for decision making that protect these rights and, at the same time, protect vulnerable patients from harmful decisions.

*Advance Directives*

One way for individuals to direct decisions about their treatment should they become incapable of making decisions is through the use of a document prepared in advance or "advance directive." The first type of document prepared in advance of incompetence was a living will. In 1969, states began to enact laws establishing formal requirements for living wills. Of the 47 states which currently have laws, twenty-five have been enacted since 1987 (Emanuel, Barry, Stoeckle, Ettelson & Emanuel, 1991).

Requirements vary in specifications regarding format, surrogate appointments, implementation and type of care permitted to be withdrawn or withheld. A recent study exploring the concerns of ambulatory veterans from a general medical clinic regarding living wills underscores their limitations. Only 4% of the patients had a living will and although 33% intended to sign living wills, 91% believed doing so would not affect their treatment (Sugarman, 1992).

Health professionals have also identified limitations to living wills. These include reluctance to believe treatment preferences specified in advance; lack of specificity in directing actual treatment decisions; emphasis on treatment refusal; and, difficulty accessing existing documents (OTA, 1987). Living wills are operational *only* when patients become unable to make decisions or communicate health care decisions *and* are terminally ill or have little hope of recovery (Clark, 1992).

Emanuel constructed a more comprehensive advance directive known as the Medical Directive (1989). The Medical Directive specifies preferences regarding specific interventions and identifies the surrogate decision maker. Treatment preferences are defined with complex medical terminology requiring professional explanation, however, and the situations described are limited to those in which there is no chance of functional recovery. In spite of the limitations, Emanuel found the Medical Directive useful for discussions with oncology outpatients. This research identified that 93% of the population studied expressed interest in completing such a directive (1991).

In general, there is concern as well as interest in all advance directives. A recent California study (Sehgal, 1992) asked 150 mentally competent patients receiving dialysis treatment in seven delivery centers whether they would want dialysis continued or stopped if they developed advanced Alzheimer's disease. The patients were then asked how much leeway their physician and surrogate should have to override that advance directive if overriding were in their best interest. Results indicate that 39% of the subjects reported "no leeway," 19% "a little leeway," 11% "a lot of leeway" and 31% "complete leeway." To improve advance directives, the investigators concluded that patients be asked how strictly they want their advance directives followed and what factors (i.e. suffering, quality of life and financial impact) they want considered in making decisions.

*Surrogate Decision Makers*

The interest in advance directives is due, in part, to the 1991 Supreme Court Cruzan decision. Nancy Cruzan's parents sought court support for discontinuance of artificial feeding for their daughter who had been in a persistent vegetative state several years since a car accident. The Supreme Court questioned the patient's parents' ability to represent their daughter's wishes adequately since they had not been designated as surrogate decision makers. The Cruzan case underscored the importance of having clear and convincing evidence of the patient's earlier wishes available to health care providers.

In many jurisdictions, adults are legally authorized to appoint, in advance of incapacity, another person to act as a surrogate or proxy decision maker. In the event that the individual subsequently becomes incapable of making health care decisions, the surrogate is empowered to act. The advance appointment of a surrogate decision maker by a patient has several preconditions. They include the assurance that the patient was capable of decisions at the time the directive was written, and freely appointed a surrogate willing to assume the responsibilities. Designating the surrogate in advance can minimize confusion and uncertainty in future medical decisions and assure trustworthy and knowledgeable representation of the patient's wishes (OTA, 1987).

According to Beauchamp (1989) the "best interest" standard and the "substituted judgment standard" should guide surrogate decision making. When the patient has left no directives or has failed to convey treatment preferences to anyone, the surrogate must rely on the best interest standard. Relief of suffering, usefulness or futility of the proposed intervention, and risks, benefits and burdens are factors which should be considered in making a decision in the patient's "best interests." The substituted judgment standard requires more of the surrogate than acting in the patient's "best interests." The patient's own personal values and preferences must be the basis for health care decisions. There are two types of substituted judgment. The first is when the patient explicitly states wishes and preferences prior to becoming incapable. The second type of substituted judgment is when the surrogate infers what the patient would have wanted through a familiarity with the patient, his lifestyle and patterns of behavior (Beauchamp, 1989).

*Legislation regarding Substitutive Judgment*

The Durable Power of Attorney Law (DPA) exists in all states and allows naming another to act on behalf of a mentally incapable individual. It is unclear however, whether the authority given under a DPA is confined strictly to business affairs or can be interpreted to include health care decision making. There are no laws or court cases to confirm the interpretation (Clark, 1992). As a result Massachusetts has two different laws: a Durable Power of Attorney for business matters, and a Health Care Proxy for health care. On December 18, 1990 "An Act Providing for the Execution of Health Care Proxies by Individuals" (Chapter 211D of the Massachusetts General Laws) was signed into law. The Health Care Proxy legislation is not limited to terminal illness but applies to *all* situations. It assures that personal preferences are honored if, for any reason and at any time, one becomes unable to make or communicate health care choices. The document allows a legally appointed proxy to make treatment decisions, according to an individual's previously expressed wishes.

Despite such procedural efforts and considerable public interest in the development of more comprehensive directives, little has been accomplished with regard to actual documentation of treatment preferences. Emanuel's Health Care Directive Model (1991), a revision of the Medical Directive, is a systematic and empirical attempt to identify patient treatment preferences.

**Factors Influencing Preferences**

Substantive research related to patients' preferences for life-sustaining technology is limited. Bedell and Delbanco (1984) found that among 24 survivors of cardiopulmonary resuscitation, eight stated they did not want the treatment and would not repeat it. Starr (1986) asked patients to consider circumstances of extreme disability and found a significant correlation between their quality of life ratings of the disability and their desire for resuscitation. Danis, in interviewing patients over 55 years of age one year after their intensive care experience, noted that "there may be a threshold of poor quality of life beyond which patients may choose to refuse intensive care" (1988, p. 801). This work concluded that 38% of the surviving patients and 42% of family members whose relatives died stated that, in the future, they would refuse care in situations of neurologic impairment, a persistent vegetative state or no hope for recovery.

Although studies which identify patients' preferences for life-sustaining care are limited, there are investigations of general factors influencing patient's preferences. Ende (1989) noted that age, educational level, income, occupation, and marital status were associated with preferences for participation in health management but accounted for only 12% to 19% of the variance. Emanuel (1991), in a survey of 405 outpatients, discovered that when asked to imagine themselves incompetent with a poor prognosis, 70% of the population decided against life-sustaining treatments. This work concluded that specific treatment preferences could not be usefully predicted according to age, self-rated state of health or education.

The OTA (1987) has recognized psychological, financial, and physical limitations as being associated with "quality of life" and has called for a more systematic method of assessing individual differences. The OTA advisory panel of nurses, ethicists, physicians lawyers and economists agreed on many fundamental issues regarding the use of life sustaining technologies for elderly persons and recommended a model for decision making that includes individuals' functional ability, cognitive function, and the right to decline any form of medical treatment. Stanley (1989) underscores the appropriateness of these components as well as the need for their careful evaluation.

In summary, patient participation in health care is limited. Factors influencing individuals' preferences particularly with regard to life-sustaining treatments are relatively unknown. Clinical, legal and ethical uncertainties surrounding their usage abound. And, the effectiveness of advance directives to articulate preferred medical treatment is unknown. Certainly improved methods of identifying and analyzing patients' treatment preferences would contribute to knowledge in these areas.

# Chapter III

# Design and Methodology

## Introduction

This chapter focuses on the design and methodology used in conducting the research. Specific areas include research design, selection of the sample, protection of human subjects, instrumentation, and the procedures followed for data collection.

## Research Design

A descriptive and correlational study design was used to examine the data. The investigation was considered correlational since it sought to examine the relationship between the hope scores and/or health status dimensions and life-sustaining technology preferences of elders.

## Sample

The population from which the non probability sample of 328 volunteers was drawn consisted of adults 62 years of age and older currently living in their own private residences within Massachusetts. This "well" elderly population was functioning at a level of competence which permitted living in their private residences without an apparent acute or confining health problem. Participation required that participants understand English.

## Protection of Human Subjects

A letter of information (Appendix A) provided to potential participants introduced the study and elicited participation. Confidentiality and informed consent were discussed as was the estimated time for completion of the instruments and the benefits of participation. Those individuals who chose to participate were given a packet of instruments. In addition participants were asked if they would be willing to participate in a longitudinal study. Those who agreed were asked to include their names and addresses on a separate form (Appendix B).

In addition to the letter of information, written instructions were provided (Appendix C). The investigator was present to offer participants assistance and answer questions. Voluntary participation in the study was confirmed by subjects' willingness to participate.

## Instrumentation

There were four instruments used in the study: Personal Health Experience and Demographic Data, a Health Status Survey, the Miller Hope Scale and the Life-Sustaining Technologies Scale.

### *Personal Health Experience/Demographic Data*

The first three questions of the survey packet for this investigation focused on participants' personal health experience (Appendix D). 1) what if any experiences may have influenced their thinking regarding life-sustaining treatments; 2) whether or not participants had designated a health care proxy; 3) whether or not participants retained a living will. Basic demographic data i.e., gender, age, years of education, religion, race, and marital status (Appendix E) was also requested.

### *Short Form Health Status Survey*

Health as a concept is seen as a multidimensional range of states pertaining to general functioning and well being. Health was measured using a Short-Form General Health Status Survey (SF-20) (Stewart, Hays & Ware, 1988). The SF-20 is a comprehensive, psychometrically sound and brief instrument based on the Medical Outcomes Study (MOS) (Stewart, Hays & Ware, 1988). Data was collected from a sample of 11,186 adult, English-speaking patients who visited providers at study sites in Boston, Chicago and Illinois between February and October, 1986. The 20 items of the SF-20 were located within the larger MOS self-administered questionnaire consisting of 75 items.

The items in the SF-20 (Appendix F) represent six health concepts or subscales: Pain, Role Functioning, Social Functioning, Physical Functioning, Mental Health, and Health Perceptions. Pain was included to capture degree of differences in physical discomfort. Role and Social Functioning were defined by limitations due to health problems. Physical Functioning was assessed by specifying limitations in a variety of physical activities due to health. Mental Health was assessed in terms of psychological distress and well-being. The measure of Health Perception tapped patients' own ratings of their current general health. (Stewart, Hays and Ware, 1988). Subscales were scored by summing the item responses, after recoding some items so that a high score indicated better health.

*Reliability and Validity.* The internal consistency reliability of the five item Health Perceptions measure was .87, compared to .88 for a nine item General Health scale of the longer version. The reliability of the five item Mental Health measure was .88 (.96 for a 38-item version). The reliability of the six item Physical Functioning measure was .86, compared with .90 for a ten item longer measure. Finally, the reliability of the two item Role Functioning was .81, compared with coefficient of .92 for the three item version (Stewart, Hays & Ware, 1988). Thus, the internal consistency reliability of the SF-20 was satisfactory.

Correlation among the Health Status Dimensions was statistically significant (p<.01). Consistent with previous research (Davies & Ware, 1981), the Health Perception Dimension correlated substantially with all of the other dimensions on the Health Status Survey. Correlation between the Short-Form Health Status measure and the demographics of age, sex, education, income and race was consistent with longer measures (Ware, 1980). These results offer preliminary support for the reliability and validity of this short-form instrument. The SF-20's brevity promotes its inclusion in studies that would often exclude functional and well being measures due to time constraints or the length of instruments.

### Miller Hope Scale (MHS)

Miller reviewed three existing instruments which were said to measure hope. They included Erickson's Hope Scale, the Stoner Hope Scale and the Obayuwana Hope Index. Miller (1986) concluded that valid and reliable instruments developed from a thorough conceptualization of the construct were lacking. The domain of hope was specified by reviewing the etymology of hope as well as theological, philosophic, socioanthropological, biological, and nursing perspectives of hope (Miller, 1986). A qualitative research study on the perspectives of hope of 59 individuals who survived life-threatening hospitalizations also contributed to identifying the critical elements of the construct (Miller, 1984). Items gleaned from these two methods were reviewed by content and psychometric experts. Seventy-five university students served as the pilot sample. The study resulted in the development of a generic hope scale for adults consisting of a 56 item hope scale with a ten item illness subscale. Psychometric evaluation of the refined MHS was completed on a sample of 522 healthy young adults to investigate the normative properties.

*Reliability and Validity.* Internal consistency was established on the revised Hope Scale with an alpha coefficient of .93 and a two week test-retest reliability of .82. The total internal reliability coefficient for the MHS was .93. Construct validity was demonstrated by high correlation of the MHS with established, valid measures of constructs integral to hope i.e. psychological well being ($r =.71$) and purpose and meaning in life ($r =.82$). A single item self-rating of hope correlated with the Miller Hope Scale ($r =.69$). Discriminant validation with a negative correlation of the MHS to hopelessness ($r =-.54$) also supports construct validity of the MHS.

Factor analysis identified relationships between dimensions of the hope scale that had the greatest likelihood of producing the observed correlation matrix of items. A three factor solution satisfactorily reproduced the correlation:

*Satisfaction with Self, Others, and Life* consists of 22 items. Satisfaction with Self is the extent to which an individual is fulfilled in terms of self competence, personal beliefs, and being at peace with self. Satisfaction with Others is the extent to which an individual is fulfilled in terms of being loved, needed, having someone to share concerns, and feeling help is available. Satisfaction with Life is the extent to which an individual is fulfilled in terms of life's meaning and being positive about most aspects of life.

*Avoidance of Hope Threats* consists of 12 reverse scored items which measure the extent to which one can cope with feelings of being overwhelmed, trapped, and preoccupied with troubles which prevent future planning.

*Anticipation of a Future* consists of six items which measure the extent to which an individual looks forward, plans to achieve goals and do things in life.

This three factor solution was congruent with the theoretical definition of hope and the eleven critical elements used as a framework for item generation. All forty items had a salient loading on one of the three factors. The primary limitation of the Miller Hope Scale is that it has not been widely tested. Its broad theoretical perspective, scientific rigor and relevance to nursing, however, are strengths which distinguish it from any other available measure of hope and served as the basis for its use in this investigation (Appendix G).

## Life-Sustaining Technologies Scale (LSTS)

Since there were no published tools developed to assess elder's preferences regarding life-sustaining procedures, the instrument used in this research was developed by the investigator. The Life-Sustaining Technologies Scale (LSTS) is included in Appendix H.

*Instrument Development.* The initial step in the design of the LSTS instrument was an extensive review of the philosophic, legal, nursing and medical literature regarding the history of choice and patients' right to choose. The concept was not defined in the medical literature. The only related and much narrower concept with a precise definition in the medical literature was informed consent.

The second step extended the literature search to include life-sustaining technologies and advance directives. Respirator, Renal Dialysis, Gastrointestinal Feeding and Cardiopulmonary Resuscitation were identified as the four most common invasive, mechanical, life-sustaining devices presenting dilemmas in treatment choices (OTA, 1987). These four devices and the components of choice gleaned from the concept analysis and personal reflection were used as the basis for the instrument.

The third step in its development consisted of group interviews of elderly people attending senior citizens' luncheons at a local community center. Participants were informed that the investigator was trying to gain a better understanding of elders' views regarding life-sustaining technology and factors influencing such choices. Participants indicated a high level of interest in expressing their views regarding life-sustaining technology, particularly as it related to life experience and functional capability. Based on these interviews and a further literature review of elderly health concerns, the investigator identified four functional capabilities as critical items in treatment choices. Each of the four life-sustaining mechanical devices was followed by four varying functional capabilities:

1. physically and mentally functioning well
2. physically incapable though mentally capable
3. mentally incapable though physically capable
4. well but with a limited life expectancy due to advanced age

Since there were no standardized tools available that reflected choices made based on life-sustaining devices and varying functional capabilities, the aim was to develop an instrument that would reflect participants levels of choices/preference on a Likert type rating scale (e.g. very strongly disagree to very strongly agree) for various items.

The fourth step in the development of the LSTS involved empirical analysis. A convenience sample consisting of ten volunteers over the age of 62 was recruited from the local community center. They were asked to evaluate the scope of the items and the extent to which the items reflected their concerns as well as the instrument's understandability and readability. There was unanimous agreement regarding the appropriateness of the selected life-sustaining devices and four functional capabilities. Respondents felt strongly about including financial capability as a fifth critical functional concern relative to decision making. "Financially incapable of withstanding the cost of care incurred by prolonged survival" was added. Additionally, the investigator observed that participants could not easily read the scale and had to continually refer back to earlier statements. Changes sentence structure and formatting were made to enhance readability.

*Reliability and Validity.* A panel of experts currently involved in clinical practice and teaching geriatrics was consulted to validate content. The panel included two hospital based geriatric clinical specialists, a geriatric day care director, a nursing home director and a visiting nurse. The panel was asked to indicate if the instrument identified health issues related to caring for the elderly and if the five statements under each of the life-sustaining technologies reflected functional status concerns of elders. There was unanimous agreement regarding the appropriateness of the selected health issues and functional concerns. The only suggestion was to put identify with bold print the functional status statements of the instrument for readability and emphasis.

Having demonstrated content validity through literature review, personal reflection, identification of the components of informed choice and empirical analysis, a pilot study using the LSTS and the other three instruments was conducted to demonstrate reliability. Forty participants, 62 years of age and older, participated. Participants completed the instruments in an average of thirty minutes with no apparent difficulty. A Cronbach's Alpha of .98 demonstrates that the LSTS has high internal-consistency reliability.

## Procedure

Representation from various community settings in nine different towns within a 15 mile radius, west of Boston, were contacted by telephone to explain the purpose of the study and request approval to distribute the study instruments. The process for distribution varied from site to site. Many of the individual sites required meetings with the investigator to review the intent of the study and related materials as well as to gain formalized approvals from boards and/or managerial staff.

A packet of material (Appendices A–H) consisting of a letter of information, directions, and the instruments was given to the potential site leaders by the investigator for review and consideration. Follow up telephone calls were made and meetings were scheduled for confirmations regarding site approval. Within six weeks, approval was received to administer the questionnaire in a uniform manner at eleven sites in nine towns. Written confirmation of the authors' earlier permission to use the Miller Hope Scale and the MOS Short-Form Health Survey is included in Appendix I–J.

Questionnaire administration took place at each site during a time which was most convenient for study participants. The majority of packets were completed and returned at the time of distribution. The data collection was completed within a six week time period. Answers were manually coded on data sheets before being inputted to computer software. Data were analyzed SPSSx for determination of Cronbach's Alphas. All other statistical analysis was performed with StatView.

# Chapter IV

# Data Analysis Results

## Introduction

This chapter focuses on the results of the investigation. Data were analyzed through descriptive and comparative statistical procedures utilizing StatView, a Macintosh statistical software program. The initial discussion addresses sampling and demographic information obtained during the study. Results of the statistical analysis for each of the research questions is then presented.

## Research Sample

In this study, the convenience sample consisted of participants 62 to 98 years of age from nine different towns within a 15 mile radius, west of Boston, Massachusetts. The data sites consisted of three retirement communities, five Councils on Aging, two flu clinics and several social and exercise forums developed specifically for senior citizens.

Four hundred questionnaires were distributed. Seventeen individuals chose not to participate after reviewing the questionnaire and 21 terminated their participation in the course of answering the questionnaire for different reasons such as "lack of time," "fatigue" and "discomfort" (pain). Even when the researcher offered to assist in the reading of the questionnaires, these participants continued to decline. Three hundred and sixty two questionnaires were collected. Thirty four participants were dropped from the sample because ten or more items were not answered. The sample under study consists of 328 participants.

## Demographic Findings

Demographic information obtained from each participant included gender, age, religion, marital status and education. Additional data consisted of responses to questions regarding personal experience affecting views of life-sustaining technologies and whether or not participants had living wills or health care proxies (Appendix D).

*Gender.* Of the study sample, 68% (*n*=223) were females with a mean age of 74.9 years. Males constituted 32% (*n*=105) of the sample with a mean age of 73.7 years. The proportion of males and females in the sample generally reflects national statistics in this age range (Pifer, 1986). The age of the participants ranged from 62 to 98 years. The mean age was 74.5 years, the median was 73 years and the mode was 72 years. For the purposes of statistical comparison, the participants were divided into three age categories (62–69, 70–81, 82 and over). These three categories permit a relatively equal distribution of the study population which is portrayed in Figure 1.

**Figure 1**

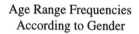

Age Range Frequencies
According to Gender

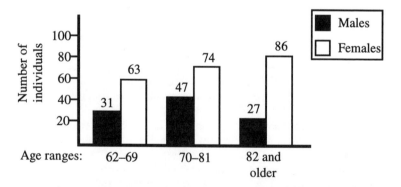

*Age.* In the Category I, 33% (*n*=31) were males and 67% (*n*=63) were females. Although gender proportions were similar in Category II with 39% (*n*=47) males and 61% (*n*=74) females, they changed dramatically in Category III. Of 113 participants in this category, 23.9% (*n*=27) were males and 76.1% (*n*=86) were females. The results indicated that there were more females in Category III (*n*=113) which represented over one third of the study participants.

*Religion.* The participants who identified their religion as Catholic comprised 48.8% (*n*=160) of the responses, followed by 42.7% (*n*=140) who belonged to Protestant sects, and 4.9% (*n*=18) "Other." Ten participants did not indicate their religious affiliation. Since there was minimal representation in all but two categories cited, future descriptions and comparisons which focus on religious preference will consider only the two largest categories of Catholic and Protestant religions.

*Marital Status.* With regard to marital status, 47% (*n*=154) of the sample were married and 39.9% (*n*=131) were widowed. These two categories comprised 87% (*n*=285) of the entire sample. The three remaining categories of "Separated", "Divorced", and "Never Married" comprised a total of 13% of the entire sample and were collapsed into "Other." The differences in marital status between males and females are portrayed in Figure 2. There were nearly equal numbers of men (*n*=76) and women (*n*=78) in the married category but more than five times as many women (*n*=111) than men (*n*=20) in the widowed category. Of the male population (*n*=105), 72% (*n*=76) were married and 19% (*n*=20) were widowed. Of the female population (*n*=223), 35% (*n*=78) were married and 49.8% (*n*=111) were widowed. These differences are important because marital status, gender and age are strongly interrelated in this sample.

**Figure 2**

Marital Status Frequencies
According to Gender

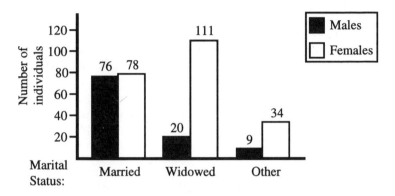

With regard to age, 68% of Category I "young elders," were married, 17% were widowed, and 15% were "other." Of the "middle elders," 53.7% were married, 33.9% were widowed and 12.4% were "other." In Category III, 22.1% of the "older elders" were married, 65.5% were widowed and 12.4% were "other." These figures support what would be expected with regard to the proportions of widowed individuals increasing with age.

Gender, age and marital status were closely related variables for this sample. Analysis of the relationships of these variables was performed using Chi-square. Results indicated that gender and age ($X^2=6.06$, DF=2, N=328, p=.05), gender and marital status ($X^2=42.04$, DF=4, N=328, p=.0001), and age and marital status ($X^2=59.03$, DF=8, N=328, p=.0001) were associated. The analysis of the relationship between age and marital status when controlled by gender, indicated that these two variables were not statistically independent for females ($X^2=49.77$, DF=8, N=223, p=.0001). For males, no statistical dependency between age and marital status was found ($X^2=10.51$, DF=8, N=105, p=.10).

*Education.* Education is a demographic variable that did not consistently relate to any other variable in this population and, therefore, has limited discussion. There were nine educational categories identified on the questionnaire. For statistical comparison, the original nine categories were collapsed into five because of minimal representation in the excluded four categories. The five educational categories and their frequencies are depicted in Figure 3. Of the 328 participants, 59% (*n*=194) had more than a high school education. Eight percent (*n*=27) did not complete high school. These figures exceed national norms but are reflective of the geography and socioeconomic composition of the representative communities.

**Figure 3**

Educational Level

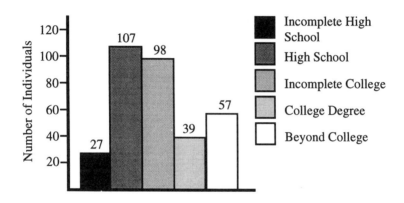

Number of Individuals

■ Incomplete High School

▨ High School

▤ Incomplete College

▥ College Degree

☐ Beyond College

**Demographics and Experience with LST, Living Wills and Proxies**

Information relative to the participants' association with life sustaining technology was obtained through the following questions:

1. "Have you had any personal experience that has influenced your thinking regarding life-sustaining medical treatments?"

2. "Have you appointed someone (a health care proxy) to make health care decisions in the event that you are unable to do so?"

3. "Do you have a living will?"

Of the sample, 41.2% (*n*=135) had designated proxies and 32.3% (*n*=106) had completed living wills. The percentage of this sample having either proxies or living wills was much higher than the 7% identified for the adult population nationally (Emanuel, 1991). The researcher further analyzed these data using appropriate demographic parameters. The percentages of participants with proxies or living wills

in demographic subgroups of gender, age, marital status and education
are presented in Table 1.

**Table 1**

| Percentages of Participants With Proxies or Living Wills in Demographic Subgroups | | Proxy | L. Will |
|---|---|---|---|
| Gender | Male | 31.4 | 30.5 |
|  | Female | 45.7 | 33.2 |
| Age | I   (62–69) | 23.4 | 9.6 |
|  | II  (70–81) | 38.8 | 32.2 |
|  | III (82–99) | 58.4 | 51.3 |
| Marital Status | Married | 29.9 | 25.3 |
|  | Widowed | 53.4 | 43.5 |
| Education | Inc High School | 37.0 | 14.9 |
|  | High School | 37.4 | 30.8 |
|  | Inc College | 33.7 | 22.5 |
|  | College Degree | 51.3 | 53.8 |
|  | Beyond College | 56.1 | 45.6 |

The data showed that more female participants (45.7%) had proxies than males (31.4%). Fifty eight percent of the "older elders" had designated proxies as compared with the 38.8% of the "middle elders" and 23.4% of the "young elders." Fifty three percent of widowed participants had proxies as compared with 29.9% of married participants.

Although the percentages of married individuals with living wills (25.3%) was similar to that of proxies (29.9%), there were 9.9% percent fewer *widowed* individuals with living wills. While 23.4% of age Category I had designated proxies, only 9.6% had living wills. With regard to education, those participants with the minimum of a college education were more likely to have living wills than those with less education.

Chi-square was performed to assess the association between the demographic variables of gender, age range, marital status, and education and the variables of proxy, living will, and personal experience. The following pairs were statistically significant (p<.05): gender/proxy, age range/proxy, marital status/proxy, education/proxy; age range/living will, marital status/living will and education/living will (Table 2).

**Table 2**

| | | Proxy | | | Living Will | | | Personal Exp. | |
|---|---|---|---|---|---|---|---|---|---|
| | DF | $X^2$ | p | DF | $X^2$ | p | DF | $X^2$ | p |
| Gender | 1 | 6.0 | .01 | 1 | .13 | .72 | 1 | .01 | .91 |
| Age | 2 | 26.4 | <.01 | 2 | 40.9 | <.01 | 2 | 2.4 | .30 |
| Marital Status | 4 | 16.9 | <.01 | 4 | 13.5 | .01 | 4 | 2.4 | .65 |
| Education | 4 | 10.0 | .04 | 4 | 21.1 | <.01 | 4 | 8.3 | .08 |

$X^2$ Statistics for Additional and Demographic Variables

**Question 1: What are the Hope Scores of the population?**

The scores were derived from the 40 item Miller Hope Scale (MHS) discussed in Chapter III. The theoretical range of scores on the Hope Scale is between 40 and 240 with high scores indicating high hope. The Cronbach's alpha reliability coefficient for this study sample was .97. Figure 4 presents the results of the total score distribution in bar graph format. The mean Hope Score for this sample was 177 with a standard deviation of 29.7.

**Figure 4**

Total Miller Hope Score

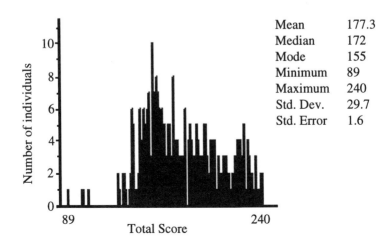

| | |
|---|---|
| Mean | 177.3 |
| Median | 172 |
| Mode | 155 |
| Minimum | 89 |
| Maximum | 240 |
| Std. Dev. | 29.7 |
| Std. Error | 1.6 |

The Miller Hope Scale (MHS) is comprised of three subscales. The 22 item Satisfaction with Self, Others and Life Subscale has a theoretical range of scores from 22 to 132. The mean for this sample was 99.5 with a standard deviation of 17.4. The 12 item Avoidance of Hope Threats Subscale has a theoretical range of scores from 12 to 72. The mean was 50.5 and the standard deviation was 11.5. The six item Anticipation of a Future Subscale has a theoretical range from 6 to 36. The mean was 27.3 and the standard deviation was 4.9.

The MHS scores were analyzed utilizing descriptive statistics. Table 3 portrays the mean, range and standard deviation for the total hope score and the subscales for the demographic subgroups of gender, age and marital status. The mean Hope total score for men (181.5) was six points higher than the mean Hope total score for women (175.3). Men had higher mean scores than women across the three subscales. Younger participants had higher mean Hope total scores than older participants (188.4 for Category I, 177.5 for Category II, 167.9 for Category III). Those who were married had higher mean total hope scores (186.1) than those who were widowed (169.8).

**Table 3**

Comparison of Miller Hope Scores Within Select Demographic Variables

| | | Hope Score Total | | | Satisfaction Subscale | | | Avoidance Subscale | | | Anticipation Subscale | | |
|---|---|---|---|---|---|---|---|---|---|---|---|---|---|
| | | Mean | Range | SD | Mean | Range | SD | Mean | Range | SD | Mean | Range | SD |
| Gender | Male | 181.5 | 105 240 | 29.6 | 101.7 | 67 132 | 17.0 | 51.8 | 9 72 | 10.9 | 28.0 | 18 36 | 4.7 |
| | Female | 175.3 | 89 240 | 29.7 | 98.5 | 55 132 | 17.5 | 49.9 | 4 72 | 11.8 | 26.9 | 9 36 | 5.1 |
| Age | 62–69 | 188.4 | 133 239 | 29.8 | 106.1 | 74 132 | 17.4 | 53.3 | 25 72 | 11.2 | 29.0 | 18 36 | 4.9 |
| | 70–81 | 177.5 | 105 240 | 27.4 | 99.5 | 71 132 | 15.9 | 50.6 | 9 72 | 11.6 | 27.4 | 19 36 | 4.2 |
| | >81 | 167.9 | 89 240 | 29.1 | 94.2 | 55 132 | 17.2 | 48.0 | 4 72 | 11.3 | 25.7 | 9 36 | 5.3 |
| Mar. Status | Married | 186.1 | 139 240 | 28.3 | 104.3 | 74 132 | 16.4 | 53.2 | 26 72 | 10.5 | 28.6 | 19 36 | 4.6 |
| | Widowed | 169.8 | 89 240 | 30.3 | 95.8 | 55 132 | 17.7 | 47.9 | 4 72 | 12.9 | 26.1 | 9 36 | 5.1 |

Analysis of variance (ANOVA) was applied to assess differences between the mean total MHS score in the demographic subgroups of gender (male, female), age (category I, II, III) and marital status (married and widowed). The differences between males and females in total and subscale MHS scores were not statistically significant at the .05 level (DF=1, F=3.1, p=.08). ANOVA demonstrated that the difference between the mean MHS total scores for each of the three age groups was statistically significant at the .05 level (DF=2, F=13.1, p<.0001). ANOVA also showed a statistically significant difference between mean MHS total scores of subgroups defined by marital status (DF=4, F= 7.2 and p<.0001). The Scheffe test was applied to detect significant differences between groups. Statistically significant differences (<.05) existed between mean MHS total scores for the subgroups of married versus widowed. ANOVA also showed statistically significant differences between mean MHS total scores for subgroups defined by education (DF=4, F=6.0 and p<.0001). The Scheffe test demonstrated that statistically significant differences (p<.05) existed between mean MHS total scores for the subgroups of those having bachelors or higher degrees versus those having high school or lower education.

**Question 2: What is the Health Status of the population?**

Health was measured by a 20 item short-form survey, the SF-20 (Appendix F), constructed to assess health status in the Medical Outcome Study (MOS). The form was designed for use in clinical practice and research, and general population surveys (Ware, 1988). Ware reported correlation coefficients for the subscales of the 20-item MOS ranging from .81 to .88 (1988). The MOS shortform includes the following subscales: pain, role function, social function, physical function, mental health, and health perceptions. Results are presented according to these subscales for the whole sample and for subgroups defined by demographic variables. The MOS scores were analyzed by utilizing descriptive statistics.

*Pain Subscale* consisted of one item (#2, Appendix F). Participants were asked to rate their pain on a scale of 1 to 5 with 1 being "Severe" and 5 being "No Pain." In this sample, 78% (*n*=256) rated their pain as mild to none, while 20% (*n*=66) rated their pain as moderate and 1.8% (*n*=6) rated their pain as severe. Mean scores on this subscale are 3.8 for males and 3.5 for females.

*Role Function Subscale* consisted of two items (#4 and #5, Appendix F ) which measure limitations in role functioning due to poor health on a scale of 1 to 3. The theoretical score range is 2 to 6. The mean for the study population was 5.26. The mode was 6, representing 73.8% (*n*=239) of the participants who viewed their roles as unaffected by health. There was a higher mean score for men (5.5) than for women (5.1) and a higher mean score for married individuals (5.6) than for widowed individuals (4.9). The younger the age group, the higher the mean score (5.6 for Category I, 4.9 for Category III).

*Social Functioning Subscale* consisted of one item (#6, Appendix F) and measured limitations on social activities due to health. Of the entire sample, 66.9% (*n*=218) had no limits to their social activities because of their health. As a result of the homogeneity of the social function subscale scores, the differences in scores between groups defined by gender, age, marital status, proxy, living will and personal experience are not statistically significant.

Mean scores, minimum and maximum values and standard deviation for the scores on the subscales of Physical Function, General Mental Health and Current Health Perceptions for subgroups defined by gender, age, marital status, proxy, living will and personal experience are given in Table 4.

*Physical Function Subscale* consisted of six items (#3a–f, Appendix F) which are used to assess physical functioning, physical limitation, mobility, and self-care. The theoretical score ranged from 6 to 18. The mean score for the sample was 14.8. The distribution of scores of the total sample showed that approximately 30% of the participants had the maximum possible score of 18 and more than a half were in the 16 to 18 score range, indicating a high level of Physical Function for the study sample.

There was a mean score difference between males (15.5) and females (14.5), indicating a higher level of physical function. The difference in physical functioning between Category I (m=15.7) and Category II (m=15.3) age groups is less apparent than the difference in physical functioning between Category I (m=15.7) and Category III (m= 13.6). Married participants had higher mean physical function scores (15.8) than widowed with a score (13.8) but this finding is clearly influenced by age since married participants were an average of seven years younger than those widowed.

*Mental Health Subscale* consists of five items (#7–#11, Appendix F) measuring the occurrence of nervousness and depression on a scale of 1 to 6 with one indicating the presence of nervousness/depression "all of the time" to six or "none of the time." The theoretical range was 5 to 30. The mean for this population was 24.5.

**Table 4**

Comparison of Health Dimension Subscale Scores Within Select Demographic Variables

| | | Physical Function Subscale | | | Mental Health Subscale | | | Health Perception Subscale | | |
|---|---|---|---|---|---|---|---|---|---|---|
| | | Mean | Range | SD | Mean | Range | SD | Mean | Range | SD |
| Gender | Male | 15.5 | 6 12 | 3.0 | 25.3 | 14 30 | 3.5 | 18.1 | 3 25 | 5.0 |
| | Female | 14.5 | 6 18 | 3.5 | 24.2 | 10 30 | 4.4 | 17.5 | 3 25 | 5.3 |
| Age | 62–69 | 15.7 | 6 18 | 2.9 | 24.7 | 14 30 | 3.8 | 18.9 | 5 25 | 4.6 |
| | 70–81 | 15.3 | 6 18 | 3.2 | 24.7 | 10 30 | 4.3 | 17.8 | 5 25 | 5.1 |
| | >81 | 13.6 | 6 18 | 3.7 | 24.3 | 10 30 | 4.3 | 16.6 | 3 25 | 5.5 |
| Mar. Status | Married | 15.8 | 6 18 | 2.6 | 25.3 | 13 30 | 3.7 | 18.5 | 5 25 | 4.5 |
| | Widowed | 13.8 | 6 18 | 3.8 | 24.1 | 10 30 | 4.5 | 17.1 | 3 25 | 5.8 |
| Proxy | No | 15.2 | 6 18 | 3.3 | 24.5 | 13 30 | 3.9 | 18.1 | 3 25 | 4.8 |
| | Yes | 14.3 | 7 18 | 3.5 | 24.5 | 10 30 | 4.5 | 17.2 | 3 25 | 5.6 |
| L. Will | No | 15.1 | 6 18 | 3.2 | 24.4 | 13 30 | 4.0 | 17.5 | 3 25 | 5.2 |
| | Yes | 14.4 | 7 18 | 3.6 | 24.9 | 10 30 | 4.5 | 18.2 | 5 25 | 5.2 |
| Per. Exp. | No | 15.0 | 6 18 | 3.4 | 24.7 | 10 30 | 4.0 | 17.8 | 3 25 | 5.0 |
| | Yes | 14.7 | 6 18 | 3.9 | 24.2 | 10 30 | 4.4 | 17.7 | 4 25 | 5.5 |

*Health Perception Subscale* consisted of five items (#1, #12a–d, Appendix F) measuring health perception. The first item describes general health on a scale of 1 to 5 with 1 being excellent and 5 being poor. The other four items are descriptors of health rated on a scale of 1 to 5 with one being "definitely true" and five "definitely false." Items 1, 12a and 12c had their scores reversed. Higher scores reflect better health. The mean for the whole sample was 17.72

## Question 3: What are the current preferences of participants regarding Life-Sustaining Technologies?

This descriptive question was answered through application of the Life-Sustaining Technologies Scale (LSTS). This 15 item instrument has a six point Likert scale ranging from one, "Very strongly disagree" with treatment, to six, "Very strongly agree" with wanting treatment (Appendix G). Cronbach's alpha was used to estimate internal consistency. The alpha for the scale was .97. Alpha coefficients for the subscales ranged from .87 to .97.

Preferences were identified for four treatment modalities: respirator, renal dialysis, cardiopulmonary resuscitation and artificial feeding. Each of the four treatment modalities represented a subscale with a theoretical score range from 5 to 30. The sum of these four subscales gives the LSTS total score which has a range of 20 (very strong disagreement with wanting all treatments regardless of functional capability) to 120 (very strong agreement with wanting all treatments regardless of functional capability). In this question, LSTS total and subscale scores were analyzed utilizing descriptive statistics. The mean total score for the population was 60.2 with a mode of 20 and a standard deviation of 20.8.

Treatments preferences were identified in the context of five functional capabilities which reflected the concerns of the aging population. They were Physically and Mentally Capable, Physically Incapable though Mentally Capable, Physically Capable though Mentally Incapable, Financially Incapable of managing excessive costs of care, and of an Advanced Age. Each of these five functional categories was a subscale of the LSTS with a theoretical score range from 4 to 24 depicted in Table 5. The mean of each of the subscales as well as the frequency of responses are also identified in this table.

**Table 5**

| Mean | | 14.8 | 15.1 | 16.2 | 14.5 |
|---|---|---|---|---|---|
| LS Treatment* | | Resp | Renal | CPR | Art Feed |
| Physically Capable | 1 | 37 | 43 | 35 | 62 |
| Mentally Capable | 2 | 23 | 16 | 9 | 16 |
| | 3 | 45 | 57 | 19 | 60 |
| 14.4 | 4 | 152 | 164 | 185 | 147 |
| | 5 | 31 | 22 | 28 | 19 |
| | 6 | 36 | 23 | 49 | 20 |
| Physically Incapable | 1 | 72 | 64 | 57 | 74 |
| Mentally Capable | 2 | 31 | 43 | 29 | 26 |
| | 3 | 95 | 109 | 73 | 104 |
| 11.9 | 4 | 97 | 83 | 126 | 95 |
| | 5 | 13 | 10 | 20 | 11 |
| | 6 | 17 | 14 | 16 | 13 |
| Physically Capable | 1 | 98 | 93 | 84 | 102 |
| Mentally Incapable | 2 | 47 | 47 | 37 | 35 |
| | 3 | 107 | 111 | 108 | 119 |
| 10.3 | 4 | 48 | 55 | 72 | 55 |
| | 5 | 8 | 6 | 5 | 4 |
| | 6 | 13 | 12 | 13 | 8 |
| Financially Incapable | 1 | 84 | 68 | 66 | 79 |
| | 2 | 44 | 29 | 21 | 28 |
| 11.4 | 3 | 92 | 111 | 98 | 112 |
| | 4 | 75 | 89 | 107 | 85 |
| | 5 | 7 | 9 | 10 | 8 |
| | 6 | 13 | 17 | 19 | 10 |
| Advanced Age | 1 | 85 | 61 | 57 | 74 |
| | 2 | 33 | 27 | 16 | 24 |
| 12.3 | 3 | 66 | 71 | 64 | 99 |
| | 4 | 107 | 140 | 135 | 102 |
| | 5 | 18 | 10 | 26 | 11 |
| | 6 | 15 | 16 | 24 | 13 |

The narrow column with the numbers one through six reflects the extent of agreement measured by the following responses: 1. Very Strongly Disagree; 2. Strongly Disagree; 3. Disagree; 4. Agree; 5. Strongly Agree; 6. Very Strongly Agree.

* Resp=Respirator; Renal=Kidney Dialysis; CPR=Cardiopulmonary Resuscitation; Art Feed=Gastrointestinal Tube Feeding

Frequency of Responses for LS Treatments and Function Subscales

Table 5 reflects data that shows that the "Physically and Mentally Capable" participants had the highest scores of the five functional subscales with a mean of 14.4. "Agree" to treatment was the most frequently occurring response for the four treatment modalities. "Physically Incapable and Mentally Capable" had the third highest score of the five functional subscales with a mean of 11.9. "Agree" was the most frequent response to treatment with Respirator and CPR. "Disagree" was the most frequent response to treatment with Dialysis and Artificial Feedings. "Physically Capable but Mentally Incapable" had the lowest agreement with treatment score of all the functional subscales with a mean of 10.3. The most frequent response to this functional category across all treatment modalities was 3 or "Disagree." "Financially Incapable" had the second lowest score. "Disagree" with treatment was chosen most frequently for all treatment modalities except CPR. "Advanced Age" had the second highest score of the five functional subscales with a mean of 12.3. "Agree" with treatment was stated most frequently across all treatment modalities for advanced age.

Table 5 also identifies the means for the four treatment modalities of Respirator, Renal, CPR and Artificial Feeding. CPR was the most frequently chosen treatment with a mean of 16.2. It was followed in order of preference by Renal, Respirator and Artificial Feedings.

**Question #4: Is there a relationship between select demographic variables and preferences regarding life-sustaining technologies?**

In this question LSTS total and subscale preference scores were first analyzed descriptively with regard to gender, age, religion, education, marital status, the presence of advance directives (through either proxy or living will) and personal experience with life-sustaining technology.

The mean treatment LSTS subscale scores and LSTS total scores for subgroups defined by gender, age, religion, education, marital status, proxy, living will and personal experience are presented in Table 6.

**Table 6**

Comparison of LSTS Subscale and Total Scores Within Select Demographic Variables

| | | Respirator Subscale | | Renal Subscale | | CPR Subscale | | GI Subscale | | LST Total | |
|---|---|---|---|---|---|---|---|---|---|---|---|
| | | Mean | SD | Mean | SD | Mean | SD | Mean | SD | Mean | SD |
| Gender | Male | 15.5 | 5.8 | 16.2 | 5.5 | 17.3 | 5.9 | 15.7 | 5.7 | 64.3 | 20.6 |
| | Female | 14.4 | 5.6 | 14.6 | 5.8 | 15.7 | 5.7 | 13.9 | 5.9 | 58.2 | 20.7 |
| Age | 62–69 | 15.2 | 5.3 | 16.0 | 5.5 | 17.6 | 5.4 | 15.6 | 5.8 | 64.3 | 19.1 |
| | 70–81 | 14.4 | 6.0 | 14.8 | 6.0 | 15.9 | 5.8 | 14.1 | 5.6 | 58.8 | 20.8 |
| | >81 | 14.8 | 5.7 | 14.6 | 5.7 | 15.3 | 6.0 | 13.9 | 6.2 | 58.3 | 21.8 |
| Rel. | Catholic | 15.4 | 5.7 | 15.8 | 5.9 | 17.0 | 5.6 | 15.2 | 5.8 | 63.0 | 20.5 |
| | Protestant | 14.0 | 5.7 | 14.4 | 5.7 | 15.4 | 6.0 | 14.0 | 6.0 | 57.6 | 21.3 |
| Education | Inc. HS | 13.3 | 5.4 | 13.9 | 5.9 | 15.2 | 4.8 | 13.3 | 5.7 | 54.5 | 19.2 |
| | HS | 14.6 | 5.6 | 14.7 | 6.0 | 15.8 | 6.0 | 13.7 | 5.5 | 58.4 | 19.9 |
| | Inc. Col. | 15.1 | 5.6 | 15.6 | 5.8 | 16.6 | 5.8 | 15.3 | 5.9 | 62.3 | 21.4 |
| | Col. Deg. | 15.5 | 5.9 | 15.9 | 5.5 | 16.4 | 5.1 | 14.8 | 6.3 | 62.6 | 20.5 |
| | Beyond | 14.7 | 6.1 | 14.9 | 5.5 | 16.5 | 6.5 | 14.9 | 6.4 | 60.9 | 22.2 |
| Mar. Stat. | Married | 15.6 | 5.7 | 16.2 | 5.9 | 17.4 | 6.0 | 15.5 | 5.8 | 64.6 | 20.1 |
| | Widowed | 13.8 | 5.7 | 13.8 | 5.7 | 14.6 | 5.8 | 13.0 | 6.1 | 54.5 | 21.0 |
| Proxy | No | 15.6 | 5.3 | 16.0 | 5.4 | 17.2 | 5.1 | 15.6 | 5.4 | 63.9 | 18.4 |
| | Yes | 13.6 | 6.0 | 13.8 | 6.0 | 14.8 | 6.5 | 12.9 | 6.2 | 54.8 | 22.8 |
| L. Will | No | 15.5 | 5.3 | 16.0 | 5.4 | 17.0 | 5.2 | 15.4 | 5.4 | 63.5 | 18.6 |
| | Yes | 13.3 | 6.2 | 13.2 | 6.2 | 14.5 | 6.7 | 12.5 | 6.5 | 53.3 | 23.4 |
| Per. Exp. | No | 15.0 | 5.3 | 15.2 | 5.7 | 16.2 | 5.7 | 14.6 | 5.8 | 60.8 | 20.3 |
| | Yes | 14.5 | 6.4 | 15.0 | 5.9 | 16.5 | 6.1 | 14.5 | 6.0 | 60.0 | 21.6 |

Men had higher LSTS total mean scores (64.3) than women (58.2) indicating more of inclination toward life-sustaining treatment. "Younger elders" had higher total scores (64.3) than "older elders" (58.3). Members of the Catholic religion had higher total scores (63.0) than members of Protestant sects (57.6). Participants with college degrees had higher LSTS total scores (62.6) than those without high school diplomas (54.5). Married individuals had higher total scores (64.6) than widowed individuals (54.5). Participants without proxies (63.9) and living wills (63.5) had higher LSTS scores than those with proxies (54.8) and living wills (53.3).

ANOVA was then applied to determine the statistical significance of differences among mean LSTS total scores of the subgroups defined by the values of the following variables: gender (male, female), age (categories I, II, III), religion (Catholic, Protestant), education (Incomplete High School, High School, Incomplete College, College Degree, Beyond College Degree), marital status (married, widowed), proxy (no, yes), living will (no, yes) and personal experience (no, yes). ANOVA demonstrated that the differences within religion, education and personal experience were not statistically significant. Differences within gender, age, marital status, proxy and living will, on the other hand, were significant at the .05 level. The Scheffe test was applied to determine the statistical significance of these within groups' differences. Table 7 shows the subgroups that had statistically significant (p<.05) differences on Total LSTS scores.

**Table 7**

| Scheffe Test on Mean Total LSTS Scores (Groups with differences significant at .05 level) | | |
|---|---|---|
| Demographic Var. | Groups | F-ratio |
| Gender | Males vs. Females | 6.12 |
| Age | 62–69 vs. 70–81 62–69 vs. >81 | 2.69 |
| Marital Status | Married vs. Widowed | 4.42 |
| Proxy | No vs. Yes | 16.09 |
| Living Will | No vs. Yes | 18.11 |

Table 8 depicts the results of Scheffe tests for the gender, age, marital status, proxy and living will subgroups for which the differences of *subscale* scores were statistically significant (p<.05). Individuals who did not have proxies or living wills had statistically significant higher scores on LSTS treatment subscale scores than those who did not have such documents, indicating more of a tendency toward treatment. Men had statistically significant higher scores than women on all treatments except the Respirator. Married participants had statistically significant higher scores than widowed participants on all treatments modalities except the Respirator. Regarding Age, the only statistically significant difference for the treatment subscales ($p<.05$) occurred between the "young elders" and "older elders" age groups for CPR, indicating that the younger participants were more apt to consider CPR treatment than the older participants.

**Table 8**

| | Scheffe Test on Mean LSTS Subscales' Scores (Groups with differences significant at .05 level) | | |
|---|---|---|---|
| | Dem. Var. | Groups | F-ratio |
| Respirator | Proxy | No vs. Yes | 16.09 |
| | Living Will | No vs. Yes | 18.11 |
| Renal | Gender | Males vs. Females | 5.52 |
| | Marital Status | Married vs. Widowed | 3.21 |
| | Proxy | No vs. Yes | 11.55 |
| | Living Will | No vs. Yes | 16.86 |
| CPR | Gender | Males vs. Females | 5.23 |
| | Age | 62–69 vs. >81 | 4.34 |
| | Marital Status | Married vs. Widowed | 4.44 |
| | Proxy | No vs. Yes | 14.47 |
| | Living Will | No vs. Yes | 14.11 |
| Artificial Feeding | Gender | Males vs. Females | 6.39 |
| | Marital Status | Married vs. Widowed | 3.20 |
| | Proxy | No vs. Yes | 17.18 |
| | Living Will | No vs. Yes | 17.21 |

The Kruskal-Wallis test and Mann-Whitney test (for binary variables) are non-parametric tests based on the assignment of ranks to scores. They were applied to further examine the relationship between gender, age, marital status, education, proxy, living will and LSTS total and subscale scores. LSTS scores were transformed into categorical variables with values of high, medium, and low. Testing these categorical variables for association with demographic variables showed statistically significant associations (p<.05) with gender, marital status, proxy and living will. There was no statistically significant (at the .05 level) association with age, personal experience or education.

**Question # 5: Is there a relationship between hope and stated preferences regarding life-sustaining technologies?**

Pearson correlation coefficient was used to assess the relationship between hope and preferences regarding life-sustaining technologies. Pearson's $r$ was .082 showing no linear relationship between the total MHS score and LSTS total scores. A scattergram (Figure 5) is used to further illustrate the distribution of these scores. Pearson correlation coefficients for each of the three MHS subscales scores with LSTS total scores were less than 0.1 showing no linear relationship between MHS subscale scores and the total LSTS score.

**Figure 5**

Scattergram for Total MHS and LSTS Scores

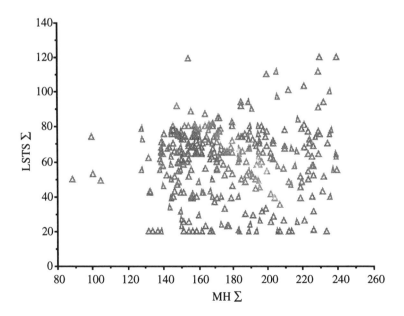

A second analysis was conducted in order to obviate any measurement disparities that may have occurred by treating the MHS as interval data. The MHS total scores were collapsed into three groups of high, medium and low. ANOVA demonstrated that there were no two groups defined by collapsed scores on the MHS scales with a statistically significant (at p<.05 level) difference between them.

LSTS scores were also collapsed into three groups of high, medium and low. Chi Square was applied to collapsed total MHS and total LSTS scores in order to assess whether the two variables continued to be independent of one another. The earlier finding of no significant difference between responses on the LSTS and MHS was supported (contingency coefficient of .07 and p of .82). Kruskal-Wallis test and Wilcoxon signed-rank test applied to these variables did not show a statistically significant association. Similar statistical procedures were applied to these scores in subgroups defined by gender, age, marital status, proxy, and living will. Again, there was no statistically significant association in any of these subgroups (p>.05) (Appendix K).

### Question # 6: Is there a relationship between health status dimensions (MOS) and stated preferences regarding life-sustaining technologies?

In order to assess the strength and direction of the relationship between the MOS subscales and LSTS scores, Pearson correlation coefficients were determined. The correlation coefficient scores (Pearson $r$) for these subscales ranged from .001 to .16. There were no statistically significant associations between Health Perception, Physical Function and Mental Health subscales and LSTS scores. One factor ANOVA was applied to the subscales of Pain, Role Function and Social Function due to their small range of possible scores. Results demonstrated no statistically significant difference (p<.05) between any two groups defined by scores on these subscales.

The scores for health dimension subscales on the MOS were then collapsed into categories of "lower" and "higher" with lower representing less health. Total LSTS scores were collapsed into categories of "lower " and "higher" with lower representing less agreement to treatment. Chi-square was applied to these collapsed subscales' scores and collapsed LSTS total scores in order to obviate possible measurement disparities stemming from treating these scores as interval data. The results showed no statistically significant association (p>.05) between any of the health status dimensions and LSTS treatment scores (Appendix L).

# Chapter V

# Conclusions and Discussion

## Introduction

The purpose of this study was to explore relationships between life-sustaining preferences and hope, health status dimensions and select demographic variables in the elderly. This chapter begins with summary statements from the research questions. A more detailed discussion of the demographic data and research questions is then presented. Finally, a summary statement, limitations of the study, implications for nursing and recommendations for future research are discussed.

## Summary Statements from Research Questions

1. The mean total hope score in this elderly population was 177. Total MHS scores decreased with age from a mean of 188.4 in the "young elders" to a mean of 167.9 in "older elders."

2. On the status of health dimensions, female participants scored lower on the Physical Function Subscale (14.5) than male participants (15.5). "Older elders" had lower physical function (13.6) scores than "young elders" (15.7) regardless of gender.

3. The mean total score on LSTS with a theoretical range of 20 to 120 was 60.2, indicating a tendency toward agreement with life-sustaining technologies. Cardiopulmonary Resuscitation had the highest mean score of the four treatments, indicating preference for CPR over Dialysis, Respirator and Artificial Feeding. "Physically and Mentally Capable" was the functional subscale with the highest mean score followed by "Physically Incapable but Mentally Capable and "Physically Capable but Mentally Incapable" demonstrating

participants' willingness to choose treatment when physically rather than mentally disabled. Preference scores for all subscales declined with age indicating a more conservative outlook toward life-sustaining technologies as one ages.

4. LSTS Total scores were higher in men (64.3) than women (58.2) and higher in married individuals (64.6) than widowed individuals (54.5). Individuals who had neither health care proxies (63.9) nor living wills (63.5) scored higher on LSTS preference scores than those who had proxies (54.8) or living wills (53.3), indicating more of a tendency toward treatment by those participants without advance directives.

5. There was no statistically significant relationship between MHS scores and LSTS scores.

6. There was no statistically significant relationship between Health Dimension Subscales and LSTS scores.

## Discussion of Findings

### Demographic Results

Within this study, 68% (n=223) of the 328 participants were females and 32% (n=105) were males. The mean age for participants was 74 years. Twenty nine percent (n=94) were between 62 and 69 years of age (Category I). Thirty seven percent (n=121) were between 70 and 81 years of age (Category II). Thirty five percent (n=113) were between 82 and 99 years of age (Category III). Representation of increasing numbers of "older elders" in Category III is consistent with national trends showing this older group as the fastest growing segment of the U.S. population. The finding that there were more men in age Category II and more women in age Category III is also consistent with national norms indicating women's life expectancy at age 65 exceeding men's by five years (Pifer, 1986).

There was an equal distribution of married men (n=76) and women (n=78) comprising 47% of the population. Of all the females, 50% were widows. Within the total male sample, however, only 19% were widowers. Again, this is reflective of national norms indicating that two out of three men 75 years of age and older were married and living with their wives, while 50% of the women were widowed (Pifer, 1986).

Regarding education, 29.3% of the total population had a minimum of a college degree. This finding, though higher than national trends, may be a reflection of the suburban middle class towns in which participants reside. Financial competence of this group, historically, suggests that the population had the resources to pursue education and continue to seek activity and socialization outside the home. Furthermore, of the participants that had at least a college degree, the majority also had advance directives (proxies or living wills). The relationship between education and advance directives suggests that education may play a role in an individual's ability or desire to articulate health care preferences and have them acknowledged. This is a point worthy of further investigation.

The most striking and related finding of this study was that 32.3% of the study sample had completed living wills and 41.1% had appointed health care proxies. Although there are no accurate statistics on percentages for the adult population in Massachusetts or the United States, the numbers reflected in this sample certainly exceed Emanuel's estimate of 7% nationally (1989) and reflect the growing concerns of the elderly about health care decisions (OTA, 1987). Additionally, the 1991 Massachusetts health care proxy legislation encouraged residents to initiate advance directives.

In this study, 45.7% of the women had designated proxies as compared to only 31.4% of men. This finding may be related to the fact that there were many more women in the older age range group and without a spouse. These women may have recognized their risk for incapacitating illness and felt strongly about designating someone to represent their treatment preferences. Such gender differences warrant further research.

Findings also demonstrate a dramatic increase with age in the percentages of individuals having proxies or living wills. While 23% of the "young elders" (Category I) had proxies and 10% had living wills, 58% of "older elders" (Category III) had proxies and 51% had living wills. These finding suggest that aging individuals are increasingly aware of their potential for life-threatening events and are determined to have their wishes represented.

Regarding marital status, of those widowed 53% had proxies and 44% had living wills. (Those widowed were also older and more likely to be female). Of those married, only 30% had proxies and 25% had living wills. These differences not only reflect the increasing vulnerability of aging people, particularly after they have lost a spouse but also demonstrate associations of widowed status and aging with advance directives.

*Question #1: What are the Hope Scores of the population?*

Past research on the concept of hope and related strategies to inspire hope in individuals focused on specific chronic health problems not maturation. Recently, the elderly were recognized as successful in changing conflicts into meaningful life experiences (Miller, 1992), and using these life experiences to enhance inner direction and assess life positively (Russell, 1989). The researcher became interested in hope as a factor in elders' ability to cope with aging and the "end of life" and decided to explore the relationship between hope scores and life-sustaining treatments.

This research attempted to identify the hope scores of an elderly population and to determine if they were related to elders' preferences regarding life-sustaining technologies. The mean score of this study population on the Miller Hope Scale was 177 with a range of 40 to 240. There are no national normative MHS scores for the elderly with which to compare the results of this investigation. The study sample's socioeconomic status, geographic location, general health and motivation to take advantage of community resources may be variables that affected participants' hope scores. Though the relationships among these variables and MHS scores have not been identified in the literature, they are findings in this investigation that warrant further research. The MHS instrument should be tested further and longitudinally to establish normative scores for different age, socioeconomic and diagnostic groups and to describe what if any changes in scores occur with individuals over time.

Total MHS scores decreased with age from a mean of 188.4 in the "young elders" (Category I) to a mean of 167.9 in "older elders" (Category III). The differences in hope scores between males and females in these age groups were not statistically significant.

Married individuals for this study population had higher hope scores than widowed individuals. This finding initially suggests that feelings of sorrow and loneliness often associated with the loss of a spouse may diminish one's sense of hope. In this sample, however, gender, age, and marital status were related. The widowed group, for example, was older and predominantly female while the married group, though younger had a nearly equal distribution of men and women. Further analysis showed a statistically significant relationship between age and marital status for women and the need for further investigation of hope and marital status.

In addition, individuals with more than a bachelor's degree scored statistically higher on the hope scores than those with a high school degree or less. This finding could be related to education contributing to elders' sense of satisfaction or increased ability to cope with life's changes and would benefit from further investigation.

The decrease in total hope scores with age was statistically significant in the Satisfaction with Self, Others and Life subscale. Scores in the subscale decreased with age from a mean of 106.1 in "young elders" (Category I) to 99.6 in "middle elders" (Category II) and 94.2 in "older elders" (Category III). The Satisfaction subscale has items which describe self-competence, personal beliefs, a sense of peace with self, access to help and being positive about most aspects of life. The finding of decreased satisfaction scores with aging is consistent with the literature which describes feelings of loss with retirement departure of family members, deaths, decreased economic security and reduced physical capability (Pifer, 1986).

## Question #2: What is the Health Status of Population?

Historically, health and functioning have been narrowly defined within the context of disease or disability, providing little information about the majority of elders functioning in the community (Nelson & Hays, 1989) or their experiences with disease and treatment (Ware 1992). Among the more recent health care developments has been an emerging consensus regarding the centrality and importance of the patient's point of view (Geigle, 1990). The goals of medical care for most patients today include achieving a more "effective" life (McDermott, 1981) and preserving function and well-being (Schroeder 1987, Ellwood, 1988).

The intent of this descriptive question was to assess health outcomes from the patient point of view with the MOS Health Survey (SF-20). The SF-20 measures basic health concepts through following subscales: pain, role function, social function, physical function, mental health, and health perceptions.

Pain was described by the majority of participants in this study "mild" to "very mild" and was not associated with any other varia The mean Role Function score was 5.26 (range of 2–6) indicating function within the study sample. These scores decreased with however and were slightly lower in women. Role function decr though small, are consistent with losses identified in the literat accompanying aging. They are supported in this study by s decreases in the MHS Satisfaction subscale score. There statistical associations of Role Function with any other variabl lack of association may be due to the fact that there were on questions about health limitations related to role function which only on "the kind or amount of work" engaged in by the individ

The Social Function Subscale had a mean score of 5.3 (ran 6) with most participants defining "no limitations." The di between subgroups of gender, age and marital status for this subscale were not statistically significant. This finding of no statistically significant difference in Social Function is not very discriminating and may be related to the homogeneity of the sample or the fact that the subscale consisted of one item, superficially assessing health limitations on social activities.

The mean Physical Function Subscale score was lower for women than men but the difference was not statistically significant. Physical Function Subscale scores did decrease significantly, however, with age. The mean score was 15.3 in the "middle elders" group and 13.6 in the older elders" group. These finding are consistent with the traditional iew of age being accompanied by decreased physical agility (Pifer, 986).

Despite the reduction in Physical Function Subscale scores with ge, Mental Health Subscale scores did not decrease. This finding is onsistent with the majority of studies in Feinson's review (1985) hich reported no evidence of decreased emotional function with age. e finding is also supported by high a mean Mental Health Subscale re for this study population which was 24.5 (range of 5–30). Koenig luded that there is growing evidence of an increased ability among persons "to cope with major life changes when compared with r age groups" (1986, p.384).

e majority of participants described their general health as "good" good." The mean for the entire study population on the Health on Subscale was 17.7 (range of 5–25) indicating a relatively ample.

*#3: What are the current preferences of participants regarding ing technologies?*

ct that more than 30% of patients in this country receiving tritional support or mechanical ventilation and 55 percent of are resuscitated are elderly, underscores the importance of fication of patient preferences regarding life-sustaining (OTA, 1987). The focus of this descriptive question was references of individuals 62 years of age and older e use of a Respirator, Kidney Dialysis, Cardiopulmonary and Artificial Feeding. The findings of this investigation ople *have* preferences with regard to their views on life-chnologies and *are willing* and able to state these e wide range of participants' responses in the findings A's recommendation to identify individuals' preferences

The mean total LSTS score (range of 20–120) was 60.2 indicating a tendency toward agreement with life-sustaining technologies. CPR had the highest mean score of the four treatments, indicating preference for CPR over Dialysis, Respirator and Artificial Feeding. One explanation may be related to the fact that people are more familiar with CPR. It is widely discussed in the media as a "first aid" treatment and is taught to the public as an appropriate response to a medical emergency. Cardiopulmonary resuscitation is understood to be less invasive and more successful than the other three treatment modalities. For this reason, CPR may be viewed more as a short term life-saving intervention than a prolonged life-sustaining treatment and, therefore, more readily agreed to. Further research into the "meaning" of CPR to individuals may be useful.

Artificial Feeding was rated as the least preferred treatment by the study population. One explanation for this finding may be that individuals can easily relate to the ramifications of being fed artificially. Imagining what it must be like not to be able to eat "real" food is more easily accomplished than, for example, not having full kidney function and requiring the assistance of a machine. Other explanations regarding Artificial Feeding could emerge from further research.

Treatment preferences in this investigation were identified in the context of five different functional capabilities. "Physically Capable but Mentally Incapable" had the lowest agreement score indicating that the majority of participants would disagree with life-sustaining treatments if they were mentally incapable despite being physically able to function. This response is consistent with the fact that the elderly, though concerned about losing the ability to be physically independent, are most fearful of mental deterioration (Pifer, 1986). As a result, the participants feel less strongly about physical than mental limitations.

The subscale of "Financially Incapable" had the second lowest agreement score with "Disagree" stated most frequently, indicating that the majority of participants would disagree with life-sustaining treatments if they were financially incapable of managing the costs of care. This finding is supported by the OTA investigation which identified the cost of care as a primary concern of the aging (1987).

Another notable finding is this study is that a number of participants gave answers of "Very Strongly Disagree" to all treatment modalities, regardless of functional states. This finding may be related to a general philosophical disagreement with any treatment that "artificially" prolongs life and would benefit from further investigation.

*Question #4: Is there a relationship between select demographic variables and preferences regarding life-sustaining technology?*

Little is known about fact rs influencing views on life-sustaining treatment preferences (OTA, 1987). The purpose of this question was to identify what, if any, demographic factors were associated with individual's stated preferences on life-sustaining treatments.

Younger participants had higher scores than older ones indicating more of an inclination toward life-sustaining treatment. This finding is readily understood. "Younger elders" are more likely to feel as if they "have many good years left" and consider life-sustaining treatment. "Older elders" are more likely to feel as if they have "lived their lives" and would rather let "nature take its course" than use life-sustaining equipment.

Married individuals scored higher on the LSTS than those widowed. This finding is in part, related to the fact that the married group is comprised of more individuals of a younger age than the widowed group. There may also be the element of "attachment." That is to say, individuals with a spouse may see themselves as having more of reason to continue on with life than if they were widowed. This explanation of attachment should be substantiated through further research. Subscales of the LSTS generally reflected similar results. Men scored higher than women indicating more of a tendency to consider life-sustaining treatment. Though males were younger than females in this population, they had statistically significant higher scores than women in all age categories. There was no statistically significant difference between men and women in subgroups of "married" and "widowed."

The most striking association regarded advance directives. Those participants who designated proxies or signed living wills had statistically significant lower LSTS scores than those who did not designate proxies or sign living wills, indicating less inclination toward life-sustaining treatment. This finding of lower LSTS scores suggests that participants who identify their preferences in a written statement or to a proxy have more conservative views regarding life-sustaining technology than those who have not stated their preferences. This finding is also consistent with the literature which describes the escalating fears of the elderly regarding the prolongation of life "not worth living" (Henderson, 1990). Retaining an advance directive is the most effective mechanism for implementing treatment preferences in an aggressive health care environment (Emanuel, 1991, O'Donohue, 1991). In this study, advance directives were also clearly associated with more conservative views regarding life-sustaining technologies.

The participants were also asked whether or not they had some personal experience which influenced their thinking regarding life-sustaining technology. Thirty percent ($n=97$) of the population answered affirmatively. Participants' responses fell into four major categories:

1. surviving or witnessing life-sustaining treatment
2. knowing someone who refused or discontinued life-sustaining technology to end suffering
3. caring for "significant others" (chronically or terminally ill) and observing their progressive dysfunction
4. attending educational forums or informally discussing preferences regarding life-sustaining technologies

Despite the fact that 30% of the study population identified personal experience as affecting their thinking regarding life-sustaining technologies, the mean differences on LSTS scores between the group that had "experiences" and those that did not were not statistically significant, indicating that "personal experience" did not significantly affect LSTS scores. This finding may be related to the survey approach of questioning in this study which may have curtailed responses. Further research into the meaning of individual experiences may be useful.

*Question #5: Is there a relationship between hope and stated preferences regarding life-sustaining technologies?*

Profound uncertainties regarding life-sustaining technologies emanate from the plurality of orientations within America and affect peoples values and beliefs about the meaning of life and death (OTA, 1987). The MHS reflects individual differences in, at least , some values. The purpose of this question was to identify hope scores and describe what, if any relationship existed between individual scores and stated preferences regarding life-sustaining technologies.

There was no significant relationship found between hope and preferences regarding life-sustaining technology within this population. Although MHS is considered to be one of the few rigorous quantitative measures of hope, the scores for this investigation were skewed quite high. It may be that the sample was too homogeneous to reflect differences in hope scores. This statement cannot be made with certainty, however, since there are no normative scores with which this study sample can be compared. This study finding of no statistically significant relationship between MHS and LSTS scores requires further investigation.

*Question #6: Is there a relationship between health dimensions (MOS) and stated preferences regarding life-sustaining technologies?*
The purposes of this question were to identify elderly individuals' perceptions of health and to describe any relationships existing between health dimensions and stated preferences regarding life-sustaining technologies. Though Emanuel's study (1991) indicated preferences could not be inferred from a patient's health status, the conclusion was based on a one item measure of health and warranted further investigation. Despite the fact that *six* health dimensions were measured in this investigation, findings support to Emanuel's conclusion. There was no statistically significant relationship between any of the MOS health dimension subscales and LSTS preferences. A factor in the lack of association may have been related to the generally "good health" of the study sample. A more heterogeneous population, including frail or homebound elders with health problems and limitations in activities of daily living, may yield different LSTS preferences.

The lack of association between health dimensions and LSTS preferences may also be related to the measurement tools. Single-item dimensions on the SF-20 had limited usefulness in detecting small to moderate differences between groups (Ware, in press). Several of the dimensions of the SF-20 were expanded to increase their comprehensiveness and precision. There are now sixteen additional items to enhance content validity and "more precisely detect medically and socially relevant differences in health status" (Ware, p.7, in press).

## Summary Statement

The primary intent of this research was to identify empirically life-sustaining treatment preferences of the elderly. Identifying the study population's preferences as well as perceptions of health and levels of hope was an attempt to elucidate individual differences in decisions about life-sustaining technologies. Although the research demonstrated that this study population of elders had preferences which could be systematically and comprehensively assessed, there was no relationship to health dimensions or hope scores.

One unexpected finding was the significant number of elderly in this study sample with signed living wills or health care proxies. This finding demonstrates the interest of this study population in a much more participatory role in health care and is supported by a recent California study (Roe, 1992) involving 59 senior center participants, 36% of whom had advance directives.

Another unexpected finding in this investigation was the relationship between advance directives and lower LSTS scores, demonstrating participants' intent to protect themselves from "unwanted" care. This finding is supported by a study showing that 40% of the physicians sampled from five countries chose a more aggressive level of care than had been requested by their patients and the physicians from the United States and Brazil were the most aggressive in the level of care they delivered (Alemayehu, 1991).

## Limitations of the Study

The LSTS is a newly developed instrument. Although the Chronbach's alpha reliability based on this sample was .96, further testing of this instrument in terms of validity and reliability should continue. A study with a time series design, for example could demonstrate stability (test-retest reliability) of the LSTS by administering the instrument at least twice to the same population at specified times. Another study utilizing item analysis could assess the extent to which items on the LSTS converged on each of the dimensions of life-sustaining technology.

Convenience sampling was utilized in this investigation and the results are not representative of the elderly population. In addition, the design did not permit detection of longitudinal variations that may occur over time within the same individual. A longitudinal study of a cohort of individuals would be necessary to illustrate the effects of time and additional experiences on LSTS preferences.

## Implications for Nursing

Many of the problems that an aging society poses involve fundamental ethical questions. There is, for instance, growing recognition that rising health care costs are due to high-technology medicine. Such problems must be dealt with directly. As questions of health care rationing take new forms, will society be willing to ration this care on an age-neutral basis? (Pifer, 1986). Can society reach consensus regarding the *quality* of life taking precedence over the *length* of life? Ethical issues like these are likely to become more compelling as the aging of the population becomes more pronounced. Perhaps one constructive way of addressing quality of life and treatment issues is to identify elders' individual views on health, hope and life-sustaining technologies.

Given the nursing tradition of respect for individuals and emphasis on patient participation in health care decisions, the profession could take a leadership role in systematically identifying individuals' views regarding health care. Nursing could empower patients to identify health options within their own framework of values and support them in defending their rights and prerogatives as health care consumers. Professional practice could be expanded to include educating and discussing with clients and their families their rights and responsibilities regarding advance directives. Since the passage of the Patient Self Determination Act in 1991, health care delivery systems are now required to recognize patients' preferences. Little has been done, however, to encourage patient dialogue and promote understanding between proxies and providers. Nursing is in the position to assume this educative and facilitative role. Continuing education and staff development programs could assure that nursing staff are informed about living wills and health care proxies and prepared to guide their patients and families in such decision-making. Intervention studies and decision-making research could be generated to demonstrate the outcomes related to advance directives.

## Recommendations for Future Research

1. The LSTS instrument identified hypothetical dilemmas. As such, the link between current preferences and actual choices is still uncertain. Consider multiple sclerosis patients for example. Will those who currently indicate disagreement with "artificial feeding" express the same preferences if they deteriorate neurologically and become "physically incapable." Research with different diagnostic groups is needed in this area.

2. Additional testing and refinement of the LSTS instrument may help to clarify concepts within the construct of preferences for life-sustaining technology. Study populations of different socioeconomic strata, age groupings and health status would contribute to understanding of these complex phenomena.

3. The LSTS scores are based on individuals' understanding and values regarding various life-sustaining treatments. A triangulation design with interview questions following LSTS completion, would provide the opportunity for elaboration of views as well as

evaluation of the instrument. Analysis of personal experiences related to life-sustaining treatments may identify intervening variables such as the length of time that life-sustaining treatments were used, the pain and suffering incurred, and the extent of involvement by the participant in treatment decisions. Path analysis could then be applied to identify the most influential variables.

4. Further qualitative investigation of the study participants who had proxies and/or living wills and scored lower on preferences for life-sustaining technology would provide rich data regarding thoughts and values underlying their choices.

5. Longitudinal research to describe individuals' LSTS scores sequentially could provide data on trends among the elderly. Relationships that may emerge over time between changing health status, advance directive instructions and stated preferences could also be explored.

6. The Miller Hope Scale warrants additional testing with the well elderly to establish normative scores and assure that the content of the instrument is clinically meaningful.

In conclusion, the arena of life-sustaining treatment preferences is an interesting one for clinical research. Not only is it an important consideration in the planning and delivery of care but also in the discussions between providers and health care consumers. Identifying individuals' preferences regarding life-sustaining technologies is an opportunity for nursing to actively engage consumers in meaningful dialogue over issues with which the public has great concern but limited knowledge. The study of life-sustaining treatment preferences and their relationship to other variables will influence client education, nursing diagnoses, interdisciplinary collaboration and clinical practice models.

# Appendix A

My name is Carol Baer. I am a registered nurse and doctoral candidate at Boston College. I am interested in learning more about individuals' views on health and life sustaining treatments. I would like you to participate. Questions you may have are answered below. If you have any additional questions, please do not hesitate to ask me.

**1. What would be required of me to participate?**

You will be asked to complete a packet of questionnaires at a convenient time. Completing the questionnaire takes approximately thirty minutes.

**2. What kinds of questions are asked on the questionnaire?**

The questions ask information about you, your health and situations in which you may consider life-sustaining treatments. There are no right or wrong answers. I am interested in how you view these situations.

**3. What will be done with the information I give about myself?**

Your privacy and confidentiality are protected. Answers will be reported as group data with no individuals identified.

**4. What will I get out of participation?**

Personal copies of study results will be available to interested participants in Spring of 1992. A separate request form is enclosed in the packet for your convenience.

Health education requested by your particular community will also be provided.

## 5. What next?

If you are willing to participate, you will be given a packet to complete. Assistants will be available to answer any questions you may have and collect the completed forms. You will have an opportunity for informal discussion with the investigator following the session.

Thank you for taking the time to read this and for considering participation in this study.

Carol Baer, R.N.
Doctoral Candidate, School of Nursing
Boston College

Catherine Murphy, Ed.D., R.N.
Associate Professor, School of Nursing
Boston College
Telephone: 617-552-4016

# Appendix B

Are you interested in receiving preliminary results of this study in Spring 1992?

Check One
__Yes __No

If Yes, please include your mailing address and return the top half of this form

Name:
Street:
Town/City:
Zip Code:

(tear along perforated line)

-------------------------------------------------------------------------------

I would like to describe individuals' views over time. Would you allow me to contact you again in two years?

Check One
__Yes __No

If Yes, please include your mailing address and return the bottom half of this form

Name:
Street:
Town/City:
Zip Code:

Thank-you again for your particiation and interest.

# Appendix C

# Directions

The packet contains five parts:

Part 1    four questions regarding your health experience

Part 2    seven demographic questions

Part 3    twelve broad health questions

Part 4    forty items regarding your own view of life

Part 5    conditions describing ability to function with four different life sustaining treatments are designed to obtain your current view

It is important that you answer *all of the items*. There are no right or wrong answers. I'm interested in *your* view.

All of the information you provide is confidential!

# Appendix D

1. Have you had any personal experience (either yourself or with someone close to you) that has influenced your thinking regarding life-sustaining medical treatments?
   Check One
   ___Yes        ___No

If Yes, please describe

_____    _____
_____    _____
_____
_____
_____
_____
_____

2. Have you appointed someone (a health care proxy) to make health care decisions in the event that you are unable to do so?
   Check One
   ___Yes        ___No

3. Do you have a living will?
   Check One
   ___Yes        ___No

# Appendix E

Please Check/Answer the Seven Questions Below

1. What is your gender?
   ____male          ____female

2. What was your age on your last birthday?
   ____

3. What is your religion?
   ____Catholic       ____Other
   ____Protestant     ____No Preference
   ____Jewish

4. What is your race?
   ____White          ____Black
   ____Hispanic       ____Other

5. What is your marital status?
   ____Married        ____Widowed
   ____Separated      ____Never Married
   ____Divorced

6. What is your highest educational preparation?
   ____No high school          ____baccalaureate degree
   ____Some high school        ____some graduate education
   ____High school graduate    ____Master's degree
   ____Some college            ____Other (please specify)
   ____trade or technical school

7. Are you employed?
   ____No ____Yes (specify number of hours per week)____

# Appendix F

Check One Box for Each Question

1. In general, would you say your health is:
   1. ❑ Excellent
   2. ❑ Very Good
   3. ❑ Good
   4. ❑ Fair
   5. ❑ Poor

   Are you currently taking medication?
   1. ❑ Yes
   2. ❑ No

   If yes, how many different medications? ___ (Specify number)

2. How much bodily pain have you had during the past 4 weeks?
   1. ❑ None
   2. ❑ Very mild
   3. ❑ Mild
   4. ❑ Moderate
   5. ❑ Severe

3. For how long (if at all) has your health limited you in each of the following activities? (Check one box on each line.)

| | Limited for more than 3 months<br>1 | Limited for 3 months or less<br>2 | Not limited at all<br>3 |
|---|:---:|:---:|:---:|
| a. The kinds or amounts of vigorous activities you can do, like lifting heavy objects, running or participating in strenuous sports . . . | ☐ | ☐ | ☐ |
| b. The kinds or amounts of moderate activities you can do, like moving a table carrying groceries or bowling . . . | ☐ | ☐ | ☐ |
| c. Walking uphill or climbing a few flights of stairs . . . | ☐ | ☐ | ☐ |
| d. Bending, lifting or stooping . . . . | ☐ | ☐ | ☐ |
| e. Walking one block . . . | ☐ | ☐ | ☐ |
| f. Eating, dressing, bathing, or using the toilet . . . | ☐ | ☐ | ☐ |

4. Does your health keep you from working at a job, doing work around the house or going to school?
   1. ❑ Yes, for more than 3 months
   2. ❑ Yes, for 3 months or less
   3. ❑ No

5. Have you been unable to participate in certain kinds or amounts of work, housework or schoolwork because of your health?
   1. ❑ Yes, for more than 3 months
   2. ❑ Yes, for 3 months or less
   3. ❑ No

For each of the following questions, please check the box for the one answer that comes closest to the way you have been feeling during the past month. (Check one box on each line.)

| | All of the Time 1 | Most of the Time 2 | A Good Bit of the Time 3 | Some of the Time 4 | A Little of the Time 5 | None of the Time 6 |
|---|---|---|---|---|---|---|
| 6. How much of the time, during the past month, has your health limited your social activities (like visiting with friends or close relatives)? | ☐ | ☐ | ☐ | ☐ | ☐ | ☐ |
| 7. How much of the time, during the past month, have you been a very nervous person? | ☐ | ☐ | ☐ | ☐ | ☐ | ☐ |
| 8. During the past month, how much of the time have you felt calm and peaceful? | ☐ | ☐ | ☐ | ☐ | ☐ | ☐ |
| 9. How much of the time, during the past month, have you felt downhearted and blue? | ☐ | ☐ | ☐ | ☐ | ☐ | ☐ |
| 10. During the past month, how much of the time have you been a happy person? | ☐ | ☐ | ☐ | ☐ | ☐ | ☐ |
| 11. How often, during the past month, have you felt so down in the dumps that nothing could cheer you up? | ☐ | ☐ | ☐ | ☐ | ☐ | ☐ |

12. Please check the box that best describes whether each of the following statements is true or false for you. (Check one box on each line.)

| | Definitely True 1 | Mostly True 2 | Not Sure 3 | Mostly False 4 | Definitely False 5 |
|---|---|---|---|---|---|
| a. I am somewhat ill . . . | ☐ | ☐ | ☐ | ☐ | ☐ |
| b. I am as healthy as anybody I know . . . | ☐ | ☐ | ☐ | ☐ | ☐ |
| c. My health is excellent . . . | ☐ | ☐ | ☐ | ☐ | ☐ |
| d. I have been feeling bad lately . . . | ☐ | ☐ | ☐ | ☐ | ☐ |

# Appendix G

Circle one number for each statement which best describes how much you agree with that statement right now. There are no right or wrong answers. The numbers refer to:

|  | Very Strongly Disagree 1 | Strongly Disagree 2 | Disagree 3 | Agree 4 | Strongly Agree 5 | Very Strongly Agree 6 |
|---|---|---|---|---|---|---|
| 1. When I ask for help I usually receive it. | 1 | 2 | 3 | 4 | 5 | 6 |
| 2. I am positive about most aspects of my life. | 1 | 2 | 3 | 4 | 5 | 6 |
| 3. I look forward to an enjoyable future. | 1 | 2 | 3 | 4 | 5 | 6 |
| 4. I am flexible in facing life's challenges. | 1 | 2 | 3 | 4 | 5 | 6 |
| 5. There are things I want to do in life. | 1 | 2 | 3 | 4 | 5 | 6 |
| 6. I am able to set goals I want to achieve. | 1 | 2 | 3 | 4 | 5 | 6 |
| 7. My life has meaning. | 1 | 2 | 3 | 4 | 5 | 6 |
| 8. I make plans for my own future. | 1 | 2 | 3 | 4 | 5 | 6 |
| 9. I am able to imagine a positive outcome to most challenges. | 1 | 2 | 3 | 4 | 5 | 6 |
| 10. Time seems to be closing in on me. | 1 | 2 | 3 | 4 | 5 | 6 |

| | 1 | 2 | 3 | 4 | 5 | 6 |
|---|---|---|---|---|---|---|
| 11. I have energy to do what is important to me. | 1 | 2 | 3 | 4 | 5 | 6 |
| 12. I find myself becoming passive toward most things in life. | 1 | 2 | 3 | 4 | 5 | 6 |
| 13. I intend to make the most out of life. | 1 | 2 | 3 | 4 | 5 | 6 |
| 14. I am positive about the future. | 1 | 2 | 3 | 4 | 5 | 6 |
| 15. I am apathetic toward life. | 1 | 2 | 3 | 4 | 5 | 6 |
| 16. I have ability to handle problems. | 1 | 2 | 3 | 4 | 5 | 6 |
| 17. I feel trapped, pinned down. | 1 | 2 | 3 | 4 | 5 | 6 |
| 18. My personal beliefs help me feel hopeful. | 1 | 2 | 3 | 4 | 5 | 6 |
| 19. I value my freedom. | 1 | 2 | 3 | 4 | 5 | 6 |
| 20. I spend time planning for the future. | 1 | 2 | 3 | 4 | 5 | 6 |
| 21. I am able to accomplish my goals in life. | 1 | 2 | 3 | 4 | 5 | 6 |
| 22. I am valued for what I am. | 1 | 2 | 3 | 4 | 5 | 6 |
| 23. I have someone who shares my concerns. | 1 | 2 | 3 | 4 | 5 | 6 |
| 24. I am hopeless about some parts of my life. | 1 | 2 | 3 | 4 | 5 | 6 |
| 25. I look forward to doing things I enjoy. | 1 | 2 | 3 | 4 | 5 | 6 |
| 26. It is hard for me to keep up my interest in previously enjoyable activities. | 1 | 2 | 3 | 4 | 5 | 6 |

| | 1 | 2 | 3 | 4 | 5 | 6 |
|---|---|---|---|---|---|---|
| 27. It seems as though all my support has been withdrawn. | 1 | 2 | 3 | 4 | 5 | 6 |
| 28. I am satisfied with my life. | 1 | 2 | 3 | 4 | 5 | 6 |
| 29. I am needed by others. | 1 | 2 | 3 | 4 | 5 | 6 |
| 30. I do not have any inner strengths. | 1 | 2 | 3 | 4 | 5 | 6 |
| 31. I know I can get through difficulties. | 1 | 2 | 3 | 4 | 5 | 6 |
| 32. I will not have good luck in life. | 1 | 2 | 3 | 4 | 5 | 6 |
| 33. I am so overwhelmed, nothing I do will help. | 1 | 2 | 3 | 4 | 5 | 6 |
| 34. I am motivated to do things that are important to me. | 1 | 2 | 3 | 4 | 5 | 6 |
| 35. I feel loved. | 1 | 2 | 3 | 4 | 5 | 6 |
| 36. I try to find meaning in life events. | 1 | 2 | 3 | 4 | 5 | 6 |
| 37. I am preoccupied with troubles that prevent my planning for the future. | 1 | 2 | 3 | 4 | 5 | 6 |
| 38. I feel uninvolved with life. | 1 | 2 | 3 | 4 | 5 | 6 |
| 39. I trust that things will work out. | 1 | 2 | 3 | 4 | 5 | 6 |
| 40. I can find reasons to keep positive about my health. | 1 | 2 | 3 | 4 | 5 | 6 |

# Appendix H

The items on the following pages are designed to obtain your current views on life sustaining treatments in the event that illness were to make you unable to communicate them directly. Each life sustaining treatment is described separately. Following each treatment, there are five conditions describing your ability to function. Circle one number for each statement that best describes how much you agree with that statement right now. There are no right or wrong answers.

| Respirator | Very Strongly Disagree 1 | Strongly Disagree 2 | Disagree 3 | Agree 4 | Strongly Agree 5 | Very Strongly Agree 6 |
|---|---|---|---|---|---|---|
| 1. Treatment with a respirator (breathing machine) for an indefinite amount of time would be acceptable if I were *physically and mentally functioning well* prior to this event. | 1 | 2 | 3 | 4 | 5 | 6 |
| 2. Treatment with a respirator (breathing machine) for an indefinite amount of time would be acceptable if I were *physically incapable of* managing activities of daily living though *mentally capable* prior to this event. | 1 | 2 | 3 | 4 | 5 | 6 |

| | 1 | 2 | 3 | 4 | 5 | 6 |
|---|---|---|---|---|---|---|
| 3. Treatment with a respirator (breathing machine) for an indefinite amount of time would be acceptable if I were *mentally incapable* of managing activities of daily living though *physically capable* prior to this event. | 1 | 2 | 3 | 4 | 5 | 6 |
| 4. Treatment with a respirator (breathing machine) for an indefinite amount of time would be acceptable if I were *financially incapable* of withstanding the cost of care incurred by prolonged survival. | 1 | 2 | 3 | 4 | 5 | 6 |
| 5. Treatment with a respirator (breathing machine) for an indefinite amount of time would be acceptable if I were physically and mentally functioning well, immediately prior to this incident, but with a limited life expectancy due to *advanced age*. | 1 | 2 | 3 | 4 | 5 | 6 |
| **Renal Dialysis** | | | | | | |
| 6. Treatment with renal dialysis (kidney machine) for an indefinite amount of time would be acceptable if I were physically and mentally functioning well, immediately prior to this incident, but with a limited life expectancy due to *advanced age*. | 1 | 2 | 3 | 4 | 5 | 6 |

| | 1 | 2 | 3 | 4 | 5 | 6 |
|---|---|---|---|---|---|---|
| 7. Treatment with renal dialysis (kidney machine) for an indefinite amount of time would be acceptable if I were *physically and mentally functioning well* prior to this event. | 1 | 2 | 3 | 4 | 5 | 6 |
| 8. Treatment with renal dialysis (kidney machine) for an indefinite amount of time would be acceptable if I were *financially incapable* of withstanding the cost of care incurred by prolonged survival. | 1 | 2 | 3 | 4 | 5 | 6 |
| 9. Treatment with renal dialysis (kidney machine) for an indefinite amount of time would be acceptable if I were *physically incapable* of managing activities of daily living though *mentally capable* prior to this event. | 1 | 2 | 3 | 4 | 5 | 6 |
| 10. Treatment with renal dialysis (kidney machine) for an indefinite amount of time would be acceptable if I were *mentally incapable* of managing activities of daily living though *physically capable* prior to this event. | 1 | 2 | 3 | 4 | 5 | 6 |
| **Cardiopulmonary Resuscitation (CPR)** | | | | | | |
| 11. CPR treatment would be acceptable if I were *physically incapable* of managing activities of daily living though *mentally capable* prior to this event. | 1 | 2 | 3 | 4 | 5 | 6 |

| | 1 | 2 | 3 | 4 | 5 | 6 |
|---|---|---|---|---|---|---|
| 12. CPR treatment would be acceptable if I were *mentally incapable* of managing activities of daily living though *physically capable* prior to this event. | 1 | 2 | 3 | 4 | 5 | 6 |
| 13. CPR treatment would be acceptable if I were *physically and mentally functioning well* prior to this event. | 1 | 2 | 3 | 4 | 5 | 6 |
| 14. CPR treatment would be acceptable if I were physically and mentally functioning well, immediately prior to this incident, but with a limited life expectancy due to *advanced age.* | 1 | 2 | 3 | 4 | 5 | 6 |
| 15. CPR treatment would be acceptable if I were *financially incapable* of withstanding the cost of care incurred by prolonged survival. | 1 | 2 | 3 | 4 | 5 | 6 |
| **Gastrointestinal Feeding** | | | | | | |
| 16. Insertion of gastrointestinal (stomach) tube for artificial feeding would be acceptable if I were *physically incapable* of managing activities of daily living though *mentally capable* prior to this event. | 1 | 2 | 3 | 4 | 5 | 6 |
| 17. Insertion of gastrointestinal (stomach) tube for artificial feeding would be acceptable if I were *physically and mentally functioning well* prior to this event. | 1 | 2 | 3 | 4 | 5 | 6 |

| | 1 | 2 | 3 | 4 | 5 | 6 |
|---|---|---|---|---|---|---|
| 18. Insertion of gastrointestinal (stomach) tube for artificial feeding would be acceptable if I were physically and mentally functioning well, immediately prior to this incident, but with a limited life expectancy due to *advanced age.* | 1 | 2 | 3 | 4 | 5 | 6 |
| 19. Insertion of gastrointestinal (stomach) tube for artificial feeding would be acceptable if I were *financially incapable* of withstanding the cost of care incurred by prolonged survival. | 1 | 2 | 3 | 4 | 5 | 6 |
| 20. Insertion of gastrointestinal (stomach) tube for artificial feeding would be acceptable if I were *mentally incapable* of managing activities of daily living though *physically capable* prior to this event. | 1 | 2 | 3 | 4 | 5 | 6 |

# Appendix I

**College of Nursing**

MU **Marquette University**

Milwaukee. WI 53233
414-288-3803

March 20, 1992

Carol Ann Baer
195 South Street
Medfield, Mass. 02052

Dear Ms. Baer:

Thank you for your interest in my work on hope.

An abstract from my dissertation as well as the Miller Hope Scale
(MHS) are enclosed. You have my permission to use the MHS in
your proposed research. I am requesting persons who use the MHS
to provide me the following at the completion of the research:

1.    The internal consistency alpha coefficient of the MHS with
      your sample.

2.    A copy of the computer print-out of the subjects scores on
      each item of the MHS so that I can continue factor analysis
      of the MHS.

3.    An abstract of your research findings using the MHS which
      includes a description of the sample.

Permission to use this developed scale is dependent upon the
above.

The instrument is based on the following definition of hope which
is not included in the enclosed materials.

> *"Hope is a state of being characterized by an*
> *anticipation for a continued good state, an improved*
> *state or a release from a perceived entrapment. The*
> *anticipation may or may not be founded on concrete,*
> *real world evidence. Hope is an anticipation of a*
> *future which is good and is based upon: mutuality*
> *(relationships with others), a sense of personal*
> *competence, coping ability, psychological well-being,*
> *purpose and meaning in life, as well as a sense of 'the*
> *possible'."*
>
> *(Miller, 1986, p. 52).*

My dissertation is available through Dissertation Abstracts
International, (1-800-521-3042).

Page   2


Please use the following reference in referring to the MHS:

Miller, J.F. (1986).  <u>Development of An Instrument to Measure
    Hope</u>.  Doctoral Dissertation, University of Illinois at
    Chicago.

Miller, J.F. & Powers, M.J. (1988).  Development of an instrument
    to measure hope.  <u>Nursing Research</u>, <u>37</u>, 6-10.


I am currently using a 6 point Likert scale to omit the undecided
option:

    1 = very strongly disagree; 2 = strongly disagree;
    3 = disagree; 4 = agree; 5 = strongly agree;
    6 = very strongly agree.

The last three items on the scale are the Hope in Illness
Subscale, which are not needed for evaluating hope.  These three
items are not part of the Miller Hope Scale.

Best wishes for success with your research efforts.

                          Sincerely,

                          *Judith F. Miller/bja*
                          Judith Fitzgerald Miller, PhD, RN
                          Associate Professor/
                          Research Scholar

                          Office: (414) 288-3855
                            Home: (414) 453-0839




JFM:bja

Enclosure

# Appendix J

# RAND

February 6, 1992

Carol A. Baer
195 South Street
Medfield, MA 02052

Dear Carol:

I hereby grant you permission to use the 20-item MOS Short-form Health
Survey in your dissertation study provided you spell my last name
correctly (Hays) -- I noticed you added an "e" to it in your abstract.
Otherwise, I might be forced to invert the "a" and "e" in your last name.

Good luck with your dissertation.  Enclosed are some potentially relevant
articles.

Sincerely,

Ron D. Hays, Ph.D.
Social Policy Analyst

RDH:keb

Enclosure

# Appendix K

## LSTS Total by MHS Col

### One Factor ANOVA $X_1$: MH S (col) $Y_1$: LSTS S

| Analyisi of Variance Table | | | | |
|---|---|---|---|---|
| Source | DF | Sum Squares | Mean Square | F-test |
| Between Groups | 2 | 206.83 | 103.415 | .238 |
| Within Groups | 325 | 140979.557 | 433.783 | p=.788 |
| Total | 327 | 141186.387 | | |

### One Factor ANOVA $X_1$: MH S (col) $Y_1$: LSTS S

| Group | Count | Mean | Std. Dev. | Std. Error |
|---|---|---|---|---|
| 1 | 108 | 59.444 | 18.667 | 1.796 |
| 2 | 113 | 59.823 | 19.422 | 1.827 |
| 3 | 107 | 61.299 | 24.077 | 2.328 |

### One Factor ANOVA $X_1$: MH S (col) $Y_1$: LSTS S

| Comparison | Mean Diff. | Fisher PLSD | Scheffe F-test | Dunnett t |
|---|---|---|---|---|
| 1 vs. 2 | −.379 | 5.514 | .009 | .135 |
| 1 vs. 3 | −1.855 | 5.589 | .213 | .653 |
| 2 vs. 3 | −1.476 | 5.527 | .138 | .525 |

## MHS/LSTS Total Col (Whole Sample)

Coded Chi-Square $X_1$: MH S (col) $Y_1$: LSTS S (col)

| Summary Statistics | |
|---|---|
| DF | 4 |
| Total Chi-Square | 1.533        p=.8208 |
| G Statistic | 1.524 |
| Contingency Coefficient | .068 |
| Cramer's V | .048 |

| Observed Frequency Table | | | | |
|---|---|---|---|---|
| | 1 | 2 | 3 | Totals |
| 1 | 34 | 34 | 38 | 106 |
| 2 | 43 | 41 | 36 | 120 |
| 3 | 31 | 38 | 33 | 102 |
| Totals | 108 | 113 | 107 | 328 |

## MHS/LSTS Total Col (Males)

Coded Chi-Square $X_1$: MH S (col) $Y_1$: LSTS S (col)

| Summary Statistics | | |
|---|---|---|
| DF | 4 | |
| Total Chi-Square | 2.058 | p=.725 |
| G Statistic | 2.081 | |
| Contingency Coefficient | .139 | |
| Cramer's V | .099 | |

| Observed Frequency Table | | | | |
|---|---|---|---|---|
| | 1 | 2 | 3 | Totals |
| 1 | 7 | 9 | 12 | 28 |
| 2 | 7 | 18 | 12 | 37 |
| 3 | 10 | 17 | 13 | 40 |
| Totals | 24 | 44 | 37 | 105 |

## MHS/LSTS Total Col (Females)

Coded Chi-Square $X_1$: MH S (col) $Y_1$: LSTS S (col)

| Summary Statistics | |
|---|---|
| DF | 4 |
| Total Chi-Square | 1.901          p=.7539 |
| G Statistic | 1.888 |
| Contingency Coefficient | .092 |
| Cramer's V | .065 |

| Observed Frequency Table | | | | |
|---|---|---|---|---|
|  | 1 | 2 | 3 | Totals |
| 1 | 27 | 25 | 26 | 78 |
| 2 | 36 | 23 | 24 | 83 |
| 3 | 21 | 21 | 20 | 62 |
| Totals | 84 | 69 | 70 | 223 |

# MHS/LSTS Total Col (Age Cat I)

### Coded Chi-Square $X_1$: MH S (col) $Y_1$: LSTS S (col)

| Summary Statistics | | |
|---|---|---|
| DF | 4 | |
| Total Chi-Square | 1.461 | p=.8335 |
| G Statistic | 1.47 | |
| Contingency Coefficient | .124 | |
| Cramer's V | .088 | |

| Observed Frequency Table | | | | |
|---|---|---|---|---|
| | 1 | 2 | 3 | Totals |
| 1 | 5 | 9 | 12 | 26 |
| 2 | 6 | 10 | 17 | 33 |
| 3 | 8 | 14 | 13 | 35 |
| Totals | 19 | 33 | 42 | 94 |

# MHS/LSTS Total Col (Age Cat II)

### Coded Chi-Square $X_1$: MH S (col) $Y_1$: LSTS S (col)

| Summary Statistics | |  |
|---|---|---|
| DF | 4 | |
| Total Chi-Square | 3.296 | p=.5096 |
| G Statistic | 3.36 | |
| Contingency Coefficient | .163 | |
| Cramer's V | .117 | |

| Observed Frequency Table | | | |
|---|---|---|---|
| | 1 | 2 | 3 | Totals |
| 1 | 10 | 14 | 16 | 40 |
| 2 | 14 | 20 | 11 | 45 |
| 3 | 12 | 11 | 13 | 36 |
| Totals | 36 | 45 | 40 | 121 |

# MHS/LSTS Total Col (Age Cat III)

Coded Chi-Square $X_1$: MH S (col) $Y_1$: LSTS S (col)

| Summary Statistics | | |
|---|---|---|
| DF | 4 | |
| Total Chi-Square | 3.419 | p=.4903 |
| G Statistic | 3.375 | |
| Contingency Coefficient | .171 | |
| Cramer's V | .123 | |

| Observed Frequency Table | | | | |
|---|---|---|---|---|
| | 1 | 2 | 3 | Totals |
| 1 | 19 | 11 | 10 | 40 |
| 2 | 23 | 11 | 8 | 42 |
| 3 | 11 | 13 | 7 | 31 |
| Totals | 53 | 35 | 25 | 113 |

## MHS/LSTS Total Col (Married)

Coded Chi-Square $X_1$: MH S (col) $Y_1$: LSTS S (col)

| Summary Statistics | | |
|---|---|---|
| DF | 4 | |
| Total Chi-Square | 2.283 | p=.6839 |
| G Statistic | 2.368 | |
| Contingency Coefficient | .121 | |
| Cramer's V | .086 | |

| Observed Frequency Table | | | | |
|---|---|---|---|---|
| | 1 | 2 | 3 | Totals |
| 1 | 5 | 14 | 19 | 38 |
| 2 | 14 | 25 | 23 | 62 |
| 3 | 11 | 19 | 24 | 54 |
| Totals | 30 | 58 | 66 | 154 |

# MHS/LSTS Total Col (Widowed)

Coded Chi-Square $X_1$: MH S (col) $Y_1$: LSTS S (col)

| Summary Statistics | | |
|---|---|---|
| DF | 4 | |
| Total Chi-Square | 4.594 | p=.3316 |
| G Statistic | 4.691 | |
| Contingency Coefficient | .184 | |
| Cramer's V | .132 | |

| Observed Frequency Table | | | | |
|---|---|---|---|---|
| | 1 | 2 | 3 | Totals |
| 1 | 25 | 19 | 15 | 59 |
| 2 | 20 | 7 | 9 | 36 |
| 3 | 13 | 15 | 8 | 36 |
| Totals | 58 | 41 | 32 | 131 |

## MHS/LSTS Total Col (Other)

Coded Chi-Square $X_1$: MH S (col) $Y_1$: LSTS S (col)

| Summary Statistics | | |
|---|---|---|
| DF | 4 | |
| Total Chi-Square | 5.629 | p=.2286 |
| G Statistic | 5.701 | |
| Contingency Coefficient | .34 | |
| Cramer's V | .256 | |

| Observed Frequency Table | | | | |
|---|---|---|---|---|
| | 1 | 2 | 3 | Totals |
| 1 | 4 | 1 | 4 | 9 |
| 2 | 9 | 9 | 4 | 22 |
| 3 | 7 | 4 | 1 | 12 |
| Totals | 20 | 14 | 9 | 43 |

# MHS/LSTS Total Col (Proxy–No)

Coded Chi-Square $X_1$: MH S (col) $Y_1$: LSTS S (col)

| Summary Statistics | |  |
|---|---|---|
| DF | 4 | |
| Total Chi-Square | .441 | p=.979 |
| G Statistic | .44 | |
| Contingency Coefficient | .048 | |
| Cramer's V | .034 | |

| Observed Frequency Table | | | | |
|---|---|---|---|---|
| | 1 | 2 | 3 | Totals |
| 1 | 14 | 18 | 16 | 48 |
| 2 | 22 | 29 | 23 | 74 |
| 3 | 21 | 30 | 20 | 71 |
| Totals | 57 | 77 | 59 | 193 |

## MHS/LSTS Total Col (Proxy–Yes)

Coded Chi-Square $X_1$: MH S (col) $Y_1$: LSTS S (col)

| Summary Statistics | | |
|---|---|---|
| DF | 4 | |
| Total Chi-Square | 2.34 | p=.6735 |
| G Statistic | 2.342 | |
| Contingency Coefficient | .131 | |
| Cramer's V | .093 | |

| Observed Frequency Table | | | | |
|---|---|---|---|---|
| | 1 | 2 | 3 | Totals |
| 1 | 20 | 16 | 22 | 58 |
| 2 | 21 | 12 | 13 | 46 |
| 3 | 10 | 8 | 13 | 31 |
| Totals | 51 | 36 | 48 | 135 |

# MHS/LSTS Total Col (Living Will–No)

Coded Chi-Square $X_1$: MH S (col) $Y_1$: LSTS S (col)

| Summary Statistics | |
|---|---|
| DF | 4 |
| Total Chi-Square | 2.01   p=.734 |
| G Statistic | 2.004 |
| Contingency Coefficient | .095 |
| Cramer's V | .067 |

| Observed Frequency Table | | | |
|---|---|---|---|
| | 1 | 2 | 3 | Totals |
| 1 | 17 | 19 | 20 | 56 |
| 2 | 27 | 30 | 25 | 82 |
| 3 | 28 | 35 | 21 | 84 |
| Totals | 72 | 84 | 66 | 222 |

## MHS/LSTS Total Col (Living Will–Yes)

Coded Chi-Square $X_1$: MH S (col) $Y_1$: LSTS S (col)

| Summary Statistics | | |
|---|---|---|
| DF | 4 | |
| Total Chi-Square | 7.911 | p=.0949 |
| G Statistic | 7.783 | |
| Contingency Coefficient | .264 | |
| Cramer's V | .193 | |

| Observed Frequency Table | | | | |
|---|---|---|---|---|
| | 1 | 2 | 3 | Totals |
| 1 | 17 | 15 | 18 | 50 |
| 2 | 16 | 11 | 11 | 38 |
| 3 | 3 | 3 | 12 | 18 |
| Totals | 36 | 29 | 41 | 106 |

# MHS/LSTS Total Col (Living Will–Yes)

Coded Chi-Square $X_1$: MH S (col) $Y_1$: LSTS S (col)

| Summary Statistics | | |
|---|---|---|
| DF | 4 | |
| Total Chi-Square | 7.911 | p=.0949 |
| G Statistic | 7.783 | |
| Contingency Coefficient | .264 | |
| Cramer's V | .193 | |

| Observed Frequency Table | | | | |
|---|---|---|---|---|
| | 1 | 2 | 3 | Totals |
| 1 | 17 | 15 | 18 | 50 |
| 2 | 16 | 11 | 11 | 38 |
| 3 | 3 | 3 | 12 | 18 |
| Totals | 36 | 29 | 41 | 106 |

# Appendix L

## Cor. Coef. for LSTS Total/Physical Function, Health Perception, Mental Helth

Corr. Coeff. $X_1$: HD(PF) $Y_1$: LSTS S

| Count | Covariance | Correlation | R-squared |
|-------|-----------|-------------|-----------|
| 326   | 9.707     | .138        | .019      |

Note: Two cases deleted with missing values.

Corr. Coeff. $X_2$: HD(MH) $Y_1$: LSTS S

| Count | Covariance | Correlation | R-squared |
|-------|-----------|-------------|-----------|
| 327   | 3.145     | .036        | .001      |

Note: One case deleted with missing values.

Corr. Coeff. $X_3$: HD(PF) $Y_1$: LSTS S

| Count | Covariance | Correlation | R-squared |
|-------|-----------|-------------|-----------|
| 328   | −.13      | −.001       | $1.473^{-6}$ |

# LSTS Total by HD (Pain)

One Factor ANOVA $X_1$: HD-2(P) $Y_1$: LSTS S

| Analyisi of Variance Table | | | | |
|---|---|---|---|---|
| Source | DF | Sum Squares | Mean Square | F-test |
| Between Groups | 4 | 2016.667 | 504.167 | 1.17 |
| Within Groups | 323 | 139169.72 | 430.866 | p=.3239 |
| Total | 327 | 141186.387 | | |

One Factor ANOVA $X_1$: HD-2(P) $Y_1$: LSTS S

| Group | Count | Mean | Std. Dev. | Std. Error |
|---|---|---|---|---|
| 1 | 6 | 64.833 | 11.427 | 4.665 |
| 2 | 66 | 57.197 | 20.041 | 2.467 |
| 3 | 69 | 58.449 | 17.774 | 2.14 |
| 4 | 79 | 63.899 | 22.898 | 2.576 |
| 5 | 108 | 60.13 | 21.624 | 2.081 |

One Factor ANOVA $X_1$: HD-2(P) $Y_1$: LSTS S

| Comparison | Mean Diff. | Fisher PLSD | Scheffe F-test | Dunnett t |
|---|---|---|---|---|
| 1 vs. 2 | 7.636 | 17.413 | .186 | |
| 1 vs. 3 | 6.384 | 17.381 | .131 | .863 |
| 1 vs. 4 | .935 | 17.293 | .003 | .723 |
| 1 vs. 5 | 4.704 | 17.128 | .073 | .54.106 |
| 2 vs. 3 | −1.252 | 7.031 | .031 | .35 |

## LSTS Total by HD (Pain)

One Factor ANOVA $X_1$: HD-2(P) $Y_1$: LSTS S

| Comparison | Mean Diff. | Fisher PLSD | Scheffe F-test | Dunnett t |
|------------|-----------|-------------|----------------|-----------|
| 2 vs. 4 | −6.702 | 6.81 | .937 | 1.936 |
| 2 vs. 5 | −2.933 | 6.38 | .204 | .904 |
| 3 vs. 4 | −5.449 | 6.729 | .635 | 1.593 |
| 3 vs. 5 | −1.68 | 6.294 | .069 | .525 |
| 4 vs. 5 | 3.769 | 6.046 | .376 | 1.227 |

## LSTS Total by HD (Role Function)

One Factor ANOVA $X_1$: HD(RF) $Y_1$: LSTS S

| Analyisi of Variance Table | | | | |
|------------|-----|-------------|-------------|--------|
| Source | DF | Sum Squares | Mean Square | F-test |
| Between Groups | 5 | 3648.615 | 729.723 | 1.704 |
| Within Groups | 318 | 136163.373 | 428.187 | p=.1332 |
| Total | 323 | 139811.988 | | |

Model II Estimate of between component variance = 10.702

One Factor ANOVA $X_1$: HD-2(P) $Y_1$: LSTS S

| Group | Count | Mean | Std. Dev. | Std. Error |
|-------|-------|--------|-----------|------------|
| 1 | 2 | 47.5 | 23.335 | 16.5 |
| 2 | 34 | 52.088 | 21.575 | 3.7 |
| 3 | 8 | 54 | 16.639 | 5.883 |
| 4 | 29 | 57.379 | 17.426 | 3.236 |
| 5 | 12 | 60.083 | 17.896 | 5.166 |
| 6 | 239 | 61.736 | 21.133 | 1.367 |

## LSTS Total by HD (Role Function)

One Factor ANOVA $X_1$: HD(RF) $Y_1$: LSTS  S

| Comparison | Mean Diff. | Fisher PLSD | Scheffe F-test | Dunnett t |
|------------|-----------|-------------|----------------|-----------|
| 1 vs. 2 | −4.588 | 29.622 | .019 | .305 |
| 1 vs. 3 | −6.5 | 32.186 | .032 | .397 |
| 1 vs. 4 | −9.879 | 29.764 | .085 | .653 |
| 1 vs. 5 | −12.583 | 31.094 | .127 | .796 |
| 1 vs. 6 | −14.236 | 28.908 | .188 | .969 |

One Factor ANOVA $X_1$: HD(RF) $Y_1$: LSTS  S

| Comparison | Mean Diff. | Fisher PLSD | Scheffe F-test | Dunnett t |
|------------|-----------|-------------|----------------|-----------|
| 2 vs. 3 | −1.912 | 15.998 | .011 | .235 |
| 2 vs. 4 | −5.291 | 10.291 | .205 | 1.012 |
| 2 vs. 5 | −7.995 | 13.67 | .265 | 1.151 |
| 2 vs. 6 | −9.648 | 7.462* | 1.294 | 2.544 |
| 3 vs. 4 | −3.379 | 16.258 | .033 | .409 |

* Significant at 95%

One Factor ANOVA $X_1$: HD(RF) $Y_1$: LSTS  S

| Comparison | Mean Diff. | Fisher PLSD | Scheffe F-test | Dunnett t |
|------------|-----------|-------------|----------------|-----------|
| 3 vs. 5 | −6.083 | 18.582 | .083 | .644 |
| 3 vs. 6 | −7.736 | 14.633 | .216 | 1.04 |
| 4 vs. 5 | −2.704 | 13.974 | .029 | .381 |
| 4 vs. 6 | −4.357 | 8.006 | .229 | 1.071 |
| 5 vs. 6 | −1.653 | 12.044 | .015 | .27 |

## LSTS Total by HD (Social Function)

One Factor ANOVA $X_1$: HD-6 (SF) $Y_1$: LSTS S

| Analyisi of Variance Table | | | | |
|---|---|---|---|---|
| Source | DF | Sum Squares | Mean Square | F-test |
| Between Groups | 5 | 1823.863 | 364.773 | .838 |
| Within Groups | 320 | 139277.646 | 435.243 | p=.5234 |
| Total | 325 | 141101.509 | | |

Model II Estimate of between component variance = −2.071

One Factor ANOVA $X_1$: HD-2(P) $Y_1$: LSTS S

| Group | Count | Mean | Std. Dev. | Std. Error |
|---|---|---|---|---|
| 1 | 3 | 38.667 | 6.658 | 3.844 |
| 2 | 16 | 58.938 | 12.897 | 3.224 |
| 3 | 14 | 59.929 | 20.963 | 5.603 |
| 4 | 34 | 58.088 | 21.912 | 3.758 |
| 5 | 41 | 58.829 | 17.152 | 2.679 |
| 6 | 218 | 61.106 | 21.826 | 1.478 |

## LSTS Total by HD (Social Function)

One Factor ANOVA $X_1$: HD-6(SF) $Y_1$: LSTS S

| Comparison | Mean Diff. | Fisher PLSD | Scheffe F-test | Dunnett t |
|-----------|-----------|-------------|----------------|-----------|
| 1 vs. 2 | −20.271 | 25.824 | .477 | 1.544 |
| 1 vs. 3 | −21.262 | 26.113 | .513 | 1.602 |
| 1 vs. 4 | −19.422 | 24.721 | .478 | 1.546 |
| 1 vs. 5 | −20.163 | 24.549 | .522 | 1.616 |
| 1 vs. 6 | −22.439 | 23.86 | .685 | 1.85 |

One Factor ANOVA $X_1$: HD-6(SF) $Y_1$: LSTS S

| Comparison | Mean Diff. | Fisher PLSD | Scheffe F-test | Dunnett t |
|-----------|-----------|-------------|----------------|-----------|
| 2 vs. 3 | −.991 | 15.021 | .003 | .13 |
| 2 vs. 4 | .849 | 12.444 | .004 | .134 |
| 2 vs. 5 | .108 | 12.099 | $6.195^{-5}$ | .018 |
| 2 vs. 6 | −2.168 | 10.631 | .032 | .401 |
| 3 vs. 4 | 1.84 | 13.034 | .015 | .278 |

One Factor ANOVA $X_1$: HD-6(SF) $Y_1$: LSTS S

| Comparison | Mean Diff. | Fisher PLSD | Scheffe F-test | Dunnett t |
|-----------|-----------|-------------|----------------|-----------|
| 3 vs. 5 | 1.099 | 12.705 | .006 | .17 |
| 3 vs. 6 | −1.177 | 11.316 | .008 | .205 |
| 4 vs. 5 | −.741 | 9.52 | .005 | .153 |
| 4 vs. 6 | −3.017 | 7.568 | .123 | .784 |
| 5 vs. 6 | −2.276 | 6.987 | .082 | .641 |

# Bibliography

American Hospital Association. (1990). Clarifying and negotiating advance directives. *Hospital Ethics*, 6 (6), 15–16.

American Nurses' Association. (1985). *Code for nurses with interpretive statements*: MO: American Nurses Association.

American Nurses' Association. (1988). *Ethics in nursing: position statement and guidelines*: MO: American Nurses Association.

Beauchamp, T., & Childress, J. (1989). *Principles of Biomedical Ethics*. New York: Oxford University Press.

Bedell, S., & Delbanco, T. (1984). Choices about cardiopulmonary resuscitation in the hospital: when do physicians talk with patients? *The New England Journal of Medicine*, 310 (17)1089–1093.

Bedell, S., Pelle, D., Maher, P., & Cleary, P. (1986). Do-not-resuscitate orders for critically ill patients in the hospital. *Journal of the American Medical Association*, 256 (2),233–237.

Beyea C, S., & Peters, D. (1987). "Hopelessness and Its Defining Characteristics." *Classification of Nursing Diagnosis: Proceedings of the Seventh Conference*. St. Louis: The C., V. Mosby Company.

Boyle, M., & Torrance, G. (1984). "Developing Multiattribute Health Indexes." *Medical Care*, 22 (11), 1045–1057.

Brody, D., Miller, S., Lerman, E., Smith, D., & Caputo, C. (1989). "Patient Perception of Involvement in Medical Care: Relationship to Illness Attitudes and Outcomes." *Journal of General Internal Medicine*, 4, 506–511.

Bulechek, G. & McCloskey, J. (Eds.). (1987). *Nursing interventions: Treatments for nursing diagnoses*. Philadelphia: W.B. Saunders.

Cady, P. (1991) *An analysis of moral judgment in registered nurses: principled reasoning versus caring values.* Unpublished doctoral dissertation. Boston College, Massachusetts.

Callahan, D. (1987). *Setting Limits.* New York: Simon & Schuster.

Cassileth, B, Lusk, E. Strouse T., Miller, D., Brown, L., Cross, P., & Tenaglin. (1984). Psychosocial Status in Chronic Illness. *New England Journal of Medicine*, 311, 506–511.

Clark, D. (1992). *Massachusetts health care proxy: user's guide.* Sharon, MA: Massachusets Health Decisions.

Danis, M., Patrick, D., Southerland, L., & Green, M. (1988). Patients and families preferences for medical care. *Journal of the American Medical Association*, 260 (6), 797–802.

Davidson, K., & Hachler, C. (1989). Physicians' attitudes on advance directives. *Journal of the American Medical Association*, 262 (17).

Davies, A. & Ware, J. (1981). *Measuring health perceptions in the health insurance experiment.* R-2711-HHS, Santa Monica, CA: The Rand Corporation.

Davis, A. (1989). Clinical nurse's ethical decision making in situations of informed consent. *Advances in Nursing Science*, 11 (3), 63–69.

Davis, A. (1988). The clinical nurses' role in informed consent. *Journal of Professional Nursing*, (2), 88–91.

Degner, L., & Russell, C. (1988). Preferences for treatment control among adults with cancer. *Research in Nursing and Health*, 11, 367–374.

Dufault, K., & Martocchio, B. (1985). Hope: its spheres and dimensions. *Nursing Clinics of North America*, 20, 370–391.

Eddy, D. (1990). Clinical decision making: from theory to practice. *Journal of the American Medical Association*, 263 (3), 441–443.

Emanuel L., & Emanuel, E. (1989). The medical directive: a new comprehensive advance care document. *The Journal of the American Medical Association*, 261 (22) 3288–93.

Emanuel, L., Barry, M., & Stoeckle, J. (1991). Advance directives for medical care: a case for greater use. *The New England Journal of Medicine*, 324 (13), 889–895.

Emanuel, L. (1991). The health care directive: learning how to draft advance care documents. *Journal of the American Geriatric Society*, 39 (12), 1221–1228.

Ende, J., & Kasis, L. (1989). Measuring patients' desire for autonomy: decision making and information-seeking preferences among medical patients. *Journal of General Internal Medicine*, 4, 23–29.

Farran, C., Salloway, J., & Clark, D. (1990). Measurement of hope in a community-based older population. *Western Journal of Nursing Research*, 12 (1), 42–59.

Farran, C., & McCann, J. (1989). Longitudinal analysis of hope in community-based older adults. *Archives of Psychiatric Nursing*, 3 (5), 272–276.

Farran, C., & Popovich, J. (1990). Hope: A relevant concept for geriatric psychiatry. *Archives of Psychiatric Nursing*, 4 (2),124–130.

Feinson, M. (1985). Aging and mental health. *Research on Aging*, 7,155–174.

Forsyth, G., Delaney, K. & Greshan, M. (1984). Vying for a winning position: management style of the chronically ill. *Research in Nursing and Health*, 7, 181–188.

Friedman, E. (Eds.). (1986). *Making choices: ethics issues for health care professionals*. Chicago: American Hospital Publishing Inc.

Gadow, S. (1983). Existential advocacy: philosophical foundation of nursing. In C. Murphy and H. Hunter (Eds.). *Ethical problems in the nurse-patient relationship*. Boston: Allyn & Bacon.

Gadow, S. (1980). Introduction: *Nursing images and ideals*. Ed., New York: S. Spicker.

Gilligan, C. (1982). *In a different voice: Psychological theory and women's development.* Cambridge, Ma: Harvard University Press.

Gortner, S., & Zyanski, S. (1988). Values in the choice of treatment: replication and refinement. *Nursing Research*, 37(4), 240–244.

Greene, S., O'Mahoney, P., & Rungasamy, P. (1982). Levels of measured hopelessness in physically ill patients. *Journal of Psychomatic Research*, 26, 391–393.

Henderson, M. (1990). Beyond the living will. *The Gerontologist*, 30 (4), 480–485.

Hastings Center. (1987). *Guidelines on the termination of life sustaining treatment*. Bloomington, Indiana: Indiana University Press.

Huggins, E., & Scalzi. (1988). Limitations and alternatives: ethical practice theory in nursing. *Advances in Nursing Science*, 10 (4), 43–47.

Jalowiec., & Powers, M. (1981). Stress and coping in hypertensive and emergency room patients. *Nursing Research*, 30, 10–15.

Jameton, A., & Fowler, M. (1989). Ethical inquiry and the concept of research. *Advances in Nursing Science*, 11 (3), 11–24.

Kayser-Jones, J. (1990). The use of nasogastric feeding tubes in nursing homes: patient, family and health provider perspectives. *The Gerontologist*, 30 (4), 469–479.

King, N. & Churchill, L. (Eds.). (1988). *The Physician as captain of the ship: a critical appraisal.* Norwell, Massachusetts: D. Reidel Publishing Company.

Ketefien, S. (1989). Moral reasoning and ethical practice. *Annual Review of Nursing Research*, 7, 173–195.

Koenig, H. (1986). Depression and dysphoria among the elderly: dispelling a myth. *The Journal of Family Practice*, 23, 383–385.

Mackay, R. (1988). Terminating life-sustaining treatment: recent U.S. developments. *Journal of Medical Ethics*, 14, 135–139.

Meltzner, H.L., Carman, W.J & House, J. (1983). Health practices, risk factors, and chronic disease in Tecumseh. *Preventative Medicine*, 12 (83), 491–507.

Miller, J. (1992). *Coping with chronic illness.* Philadelphia, Pa: F.A. Davis.

Miller, J. (1986). *Development of an instrument to measure hope.* Unpublished doctoral dissertation. University of Illinois, Chicago.

Miller, J., & Powers, M. (1988). Development of an instrument to measure hope. *Nursing Research*, 37 (1), 6–10.

Miller, T., & Cugliari, A.M. (1990). Withdrawing and withholding treatment: policies in long term care facilities. *The Gerontologist*, 30 (4),462–468.

Murphy, C.D., & Hunter, H. (Eds.). (1983). *Ethical problems in the nurse patient relationship.* Boston, Ma.: Bouron Allyn and Bacon Publishing Co.

Moinpour, C. & Teigl, P. (1989). Quality of life end points in cancer clinical trials: review and recommendations. *Journal of the National Cancer Institute*, 81(7), 485–495.

Nelson, E., Hays, R., Arnold, S., Kwoh, K. & Sherbourne, C. (1989). *Age and functional health states.* Santa Monica, Ca: Rand Corporation.

Ouslander, J., Tymechuk, A. & Rahbar, B. (1989). Health care decisions among elderly long-term care residents and their potential proxies. *Archives of Internal Medicine,* 149,1367–1372.

Parkerson, G., Gehlbach, S., Wagner, E., James, S. & Clapp. (1981). The Duke-UNC health profile: an adult health status instrument for primary care. *Medical Care,* 19, 806–828.

Parse, R. (1981). *Man-living health. A theory of nursing.* New York: J. Wiley & Sons.

Paterson, J. & Zderad, L. (1988). *Humanistic nursing.* New York: National League for Nursing.

Patrick, D.L. & Bergner, M. (1990) Measurement of health status in the 1990's. *Annual Review of Public Health,* 11, 165–183.

Pifer, A. & Bronte, L.(Eds.). (1986). *Our aging society: paradox and promise.*

New York: W. W. Norton & Company.

President's Commission for the Study of Ethical Problems in Medicine and Biomedical and Behavioral Research. (1981, 1982, 1983). *Reports, Proceedings and Appendices.* Washington, D.C.: U.S. Government Printing Office.

President's Commission for the Study of Ethical Problems in Medicine and Biomedical and Behavioral Research. (1983). *Deciding to forgo life sustaining treatment.* Washington, D.C.: U.S. Government Printing Office.

Rice, D. & Cugliani (1980). Health Status of American Woman. *Woman and Health,* 5, 5–22.

Roe, J., Goldstein, M., Massey,K., & Pascoe, D. (1992). Durable power of attorney for health care: a survey of senior center participants. *Archives of Internal Medicine,* 152, (2), 259–261.

Schacht, E. (1989). Comment to the editors regarding normative judgments and personal preferences. *Journal of General Internal Medicine,* 4, 360–361.

Schneiderman, L. Jecker, N. & Jonsen, A. (1990). Medical futility: its meaning and ethical implications. *Annals of Internal Medicine,* 112 (12), 949–954.

Sehgal, A., Galbraith, A., Chesney, M., Schoenfeld, P. Charles, G., & Lo-B (1992). How strictly do dialysis patients want their advance directives followed? *Journal of the American Medical Association,* 267 (1), 59–63.

Shelley, S., Zahorchak, M., & Gambrill, C. (1987). Aggressiveness of nursing care for older patients and those with do-not-resuscitate orders. *Nursing Research,* 36 (3),157–162.

Stanley, J. (1989). The appleton consensus: suggested international guidelines for decisions to forego medical treatment. *Journal of Medical Ethics,* 15, 129–136.

Starr, T.J., Pearlman, R.A. & Uhlmann. (1986). Quality of life and resuscitation decisions in elderly patients. *Journal of General Internal Medicine,* 1 (6), 373–379.

Stewart, A., Hays, R., & Ware, J. (1988). The MOS Short-form general health survey. *Medical Care,* 26 (7), 724–732.

Stoll, B. (1990). Choosing between cancer patients. *Journal of Medical Ethics,* 16, 71–74.

Sugarman, J. Weinberger, M., & Samsa, G. (1992). Factors associated with veterans' decisions about living wills. *Archives of Internal Medicine,* 152 (2) 343–347.

Trice, L. (1990). Meaningful life experience to the elderly. *Image,*22 (4), 248–251.

U.S. Congress, Office of Technology Assessment. (1988). *Institutional protocols for decisions about life-sustaining treatments.* OTA-BA-389. Washington, D.C.: U.S. Gov. Printing Office.

U.S. Congress, Office of Technology Assessment. (1987). *Life-sustaining technologies and the elderly,* OTA-BA-306. Washington, D.C.: U.S. Gov. Printing Office.

U.S. Department of Health and Human Services. (1989). Aging in the eighties: the prevalence of comorbidity and its association with disability. *Advance Data,* 170, 1–8.

Watson, J. (1985). *Nursing: human science and human care.* Norwalk, Ct: Appleton-Century-Crofts.

Ware, J. (In Press). The use of health status and quality of life measures in outcomes and effectiveness research.

Wright, R. (1987). *Human values in health care: the practice of ethics.* New York: McGraw-Hill.

Yeo, M. (1989). Integration of nursing theory and nursing ethics. *Advances in Nursing Science*, 2 (3), 33–42.

Zimmerman, J., Knasu, W., Sharpe, S., Anderson, A., Draper, A., & Wagner, D. (1986). The use and implications of do not resuscitate orders in intensive care units. *Journal of the American Medical Association*, 255 (3), 351–356.

# Index